# HOW TO *WIN*
# AT
# *PINOCHLE*
## AND OTHER GAMES

*including*

# GIN RUMMY — RED DOG
# BLACK JACK

**KEY PUBLISHING COMPANY** • **New York, N. Y.**

Printed in the United States of America

# TABLE OF CONTENTS

Chapter      Page

I. PINOCHLE SIMPLIFIED    1

The Pinochle Pack — The Melds — The Trump Sequence — Aces — Kings — Queens — Jacks — Marriages — The Dix — Pinochle: Simple — Grand — Double. Styles of Count: Original — Simplified — Compromise. The Best Count to Use. Other comments.

II. MELD, DRAW AND PLAY    9

Essential facts in Pinochle — Sample Melds — Highest Possible Meld (in Auction with Widow) — Best scoring hand — The "Perfect" Hand — Groups of Melds.

III. AUCTION PINOCHLE    17

Most popular form — Auction With Widow — Number of Players — Dealing the Cards — Improved Deal — Bidding the Hands — Minimum Bids — Declaring the Meld — The Discard — Examples of Discard — Play of the Hand — Adding the Count — Different Methods — Object of Game — Spades Double — Hearts Triple. Counts Reviewed.

IV. HOW TO BID AND WIN    27

Discussion of "safe" play. Adding "losers" — The wrong way — the right way. The Sound Bid — Sample Hand with Widow possibilities — Another sample — Spotting freak hands — Allowing leeway — Three-handed Pinochle.

V. BIDDING THE LIMIT    37

Question of profits — The Limit Bid System — Potential Values — Numerous examples — Three "spots" open — Buried counters. Watch out for Freak Hands!

VI.    BIDDING BEYOND THE LIMIT                           45

The Risk Bid — When to use it — Pitfalls to avoid — The
Wild Bid — Used with the Bluff Bid — The Best Bluff
Hand. Partnership Pinochle.

VII.    HOW TO PLAY THE HAND                            51

An Ideal Hand — How to play it — Common type — Its
logical play — A Balanced Hand — Angles on play —
When to switch. Playing Against Bidder — Watching
counters — Other pointers.

VIII.    TWO-HANDED PINOCHLE                            57

The Original Game — Examples of play — Leads and
sacrifices — When to vary the play — Matters of Meld.

IX.    RUMMY AND GIN RUMMY                            65

The basic game — Sample hands — The Meld factor —
Gin Rummy — To Knock or Not — Watching the Opponent — High or Low Cards — Making "dead" discards.

X.    RED DOG AND BLACK JACK                          75

Rules of Red Dog — How to bet — A question of limit —
Increasing the average — Black Jack, or Twenty-one —
Going bust — When to Stay — The Game of Seven and a
Half — Similarity to Black Jack — Special Features

XI.    HOW CHEATS CAN TRIM YOU                        85

Card cheats analyzed — Marked Cards in Pinochle — Easy
Marks — Dealing Yourself Out — The Old Army Game
— Gin, the Cheater's Delight — Push Button Cheating —
The Second Deal — Shiners.

# Chapter I

## PINOCHLE SIMPLIFIED

The name "Pinochle" is applied to a group of card games which have certain basic features in common, but from there on, the similarity ceases. This has caused much confusion, not only in the play but in the description of the game, or games, to be correct.

Certain rules or procedures have been interchanged with total disregard of the fact that the games, as well as their purposes, are fundamentally different. Also, it has been customary to explain several of the games, or at least their principal variants, under a single head. This not only adds complications; it justifies the very misconcepts that should be avoided.

Actually, there is nearly as much difference between Auction Pinochle and Two-Handed Pinochle as there is between such highly unrelated games as Poker and Casino. Auction Pinochle, is often dominated by the "meld," a type of "showdown" somewhat like Poker; whereas Two-Handed Pinochle, though it also features melds, requires the taking of tricks with an ever-diminishing pack, a la Casino.

Such differences will be discussed under the headings of the games themselves. At present, let us consider the features peculiar to all forms of pinochle.

First: The Pinochle Pack

This consists of 48 cards, from Ace down to Nine in each suit—Spades, Hearts, Clubs, Diamonds—with each card duplicated. The Ten ranks next to the Ace in value; the remaining cards run King, Queen, Jack, Nine, thus:

| | | | | | | | | | | | |
|---|---|---|---|---|---|---|---|---|---|---|---|
| A♠ | A♠ | 10♠ | 10♠ | K♠ | K♠ | Q♠ | Q♠ | J♠ | J♠ | 9♠ | 9♠ |
| A♡ | A♡ | 10♡ | 10♡ | K♡ | K♡ | Q♡ | Q♡ | J♡ | J♡ | 9♡ | 9♡ |
| A♣ | A♣ | 10♣ | 10♣ | K♣ | K♣ | Q♣ | Q♣ | J♣ | J♣ | 9♣ | 9♣ |
| A♦ | A♦ | 10♦ | 10♦ | K♦ | K♦ | Q♦ | Q♦ | J♦ | J♦ | 9♦ | 9♦ |

In play, one suit is always Trumps, so that a card of that suit wins or "takes" a trick, when played upon cards of other suits. Otherwise, the card of highest value takes the trick, according to whatever suit is led.

1

The question of duplicates is easily decided: If two identical **cards** appear in the same trick, the one first played takes precedence over its twin and wins the trick. Thus, a player leading the Ace of Hearts would capture the other Ace of Hearts, should a subsequent player drop it on that trick.

In Pinochle, hands of 12 to 16 cards are dealt to each player, according to the number playing in the game, or the type of game itself. The hands are played and tricks are taken, as in Bridge, Five Hundred and such games. But in Pinochle, before playing his cards, a player has a chance to "meld" them; that is, he may declare or show cards that form certain combinations, which count toward his total score. This is Number Two in our list of features:

Second, The Meld and its Values.

In the meld, we find not only the most important but the most interesting phase of Pinochle. Here, the game has the fascination of Poker, in which certain combinations of cards take precedence over others. But in Pinochle, this "showdown" is strictly a matter of values.

Tops among Pinochle melds is:

### THE TRUMP SEQUENCE

This combination, more simply called a "Sequence" and also known as a "Run" or a "Flush," consists of the Ace, 10, King, Queen, Jack of the suit which is declared Trumps.

$$A \spadesuit \quad 10 \spadesuit \quad K \spadesuit \quad Q \spadesuit \quad J \spadesuit \quad 9 \spadesuit$$

The name "Trump Sequence" is preferable for this meld, because the suit *must* be Trump, otherwise the "Run" does not count. This, of course, makes it more difficult to obtain, but do not be discouraged.

Since there are two of each card in the Pinochle pack, a Sequence may show up quite frequently. When it does, it counts: 150 Points.

Next in value comes the combination known as:

### ONE HUNDRED ACES

Actually, this meld consists of Four Aces, each of a different suit, as shown:

$$A \spadesuit \quad A \heartsuit \quad A \clubsuit \quad A \diamondsuit$$

The term "100 Aces" refers to the value, or count of the combination, namely: 100 Points.

Next in value come:

## EIGHTY KINGS

This meld is composed of Four Kings, one from each suit. It scores less than Four Aces, but has more possibilities of linking with other combinations.

K♠ K♡ K♣ K♢

Again, the term "80" refers to the value where Kings are concerned. They count: 80 points.

Next in order:

## SIXTY QUEENS

Four Queens, each of a different suit:

Q♠ Q♡ Q♣ Q♢

As hard to acquire as Aces or Kings, but valued less. Like Kings, Queens are valuable in other combinations. They count: 60 points.

Next in this group come:

## FORTY JACKS

Popularly known as the "Boys from Brooklyn," this combination is the lowest in value of its type.

J♠ J♡ J♣ J♢

The Four Jacks count: 40 Points.

Another type of meld, in fact the combinations which appear most frequently, are the

## MARRIAGES

which consist simply of the King and Queen of any suit. These are so easy to obtain, that a player may often have two Marriages of the same suit and occasionally he may hold a complete set of all suits:

K♠ K♡ K♣ K♢
Q♠ Q♡ Q♣ Q♢

A Marriage in the Trump Suit has double value over the others and is called a Royal Marriage. In scoring:

Royal Marriages count 40 Points
Other Marriages count 20 Points

## THE DIX (or DEECE)

This is simply the Nine Spot of the Trump Suit, which we assume in this case to be Spades.

9♠

The name "Dix" comes from the French word meaning "ten" and is pronounced "Deece." You guessed it. The Dix counts 10 Points.

## PINOCHLE

This is a special Meld from which the game "Pinochle" derives its name:

J◇   Q♠

A simple Pinochle counts 40 Points.

## GRAND PINOCHLE

This combines a Marriage (in Spades) with a simple Pinochle, thus:

K♠   Q♠   J◇

Once this combo rated a special value of 80 Points. It still does, but only when Spades are trump, making the King and Queen a Royal Marriage. So:

> With Spades as Trump, it counts 80 Points.
> With another Trump Suit, it counts 60 Points.

## DOUBLE PINOCHLE

This consists of both Jacks of Diamonds along with the two Queens of Spades:

J◇   Q♠    J◇   Q♠

Since the player must hold all four cards that compose two "Pinochles" this is a rather difficult combination to acquire and as a result, it was valued at 300 Points in old-time Pinochle games. In modern play, no special bonus is given to the combination.

Double Pinochle counts 80.

It is quite possible to combine cards from different melds with others to form a meld of a different type; in fact, the procedure is recommended and becomes one of the most intriguing features of the game.

For example: The Ace of Trump can figure both in a Sequence and in a Hundred Aces. Similarly, the King, Queen, Jack of Trumps may be part of Eighty Kings, Sixty Queens or Forty Jacks, respectively.

Another type of meld which definitely must be rated or considered in its own right is:

## THE ROUND TRIP

also known as a "Roundhouse," this combination consists of Four Kings and Four Queens, all of different suits, thereby incorporating six melds in one:

$$K\spadesuit \quad K\heartsuit \quad K\clubsuit \quad K\diamondsuit$$
$$Q\spadesuit \quad Q\heartsuit \quad Q\clubsuit \quad Q\diamondsuit$$

The six counting units are Eighty Kings (80) and Sixty Queens (60) along with a Royal Marriage (40) and three other Marriages (20 each) which are added to make the grand total. A Round Trip counts 240.

Since this score is quite obvious, many players wonder why a Round Trip is considered as a special Meld. In some circles, it was once counted as 250 instead of 240, but that practice was either rare or localized.

The real reason why the Round Trip should be included in every List of Melds is this:

Each Meld must be formed by the addition of a new card or cards, making it a continuous process as the player announces each succeeding combination.

If he has melded Eighty Kings and Sixty Queens, he can't just separate them into pairs and call them four Marriages. In Pinochle practice, he should add another King to each Queen, or vice versa, to make the Marriages count.

Or, he might declare the Marriages first; then add an odd King to make 80 and an odd Queen to score 60. But either way, he couldn't cash in his full 240 with just four Kings and four Queens.

That problem still crops up in Two-Handed Pinochle but in Auction and other modern forms of the game, the Roundhouse solves the difficulty. When the Round Trip first came into vogue does not matter, but its purpose should not be overlooked, as it furnishes an important key to the whole process of melding, which will be discussed in the next chapter.

Meanwhile, there is another feature to consider:

Third, Scoring in the Play.

In Pinochle, it is not the number of tricks the player takes, but the points represented by certain cards that are won in the course of play. These "counters" as they are called, add up to 240 points, plus an additional 10 for taking the final trick.

Any points so made are added to the score that was picked up from the Meld. That leaves only the question: What cards are counters? This can be answered in three ways, namely by:

## THE ORIGINAL COUNT

This type of count, still used by inveterate Pinochle players today, gives values to all cards except the Nines and cuts the play to a fine point that can produce some real hair-breadth results.

The cards are valued thus:

| | |
|---|---|
| Each ACE counts | 11 Points |
| Each TEN counts | 10 Points |
| Each KING counts | 4 Points |
| Each QUEEN counts | 3 Points |
| Each JACK counts | 2 Points |
| Total | 30 |
| Times 8 (of each type) | 240 |
| Plus LAST TRICK | 10 |
| TOTAL | 250 |

This count shows why Pinochle is scored in "tens" instead of "units." If all scores were reduced to 1/10, so that a Sequence rated 15, Four Aces 10, a Marriage 2 and so on, the Original Count would become fractional. That disadvantage—if it can be called such—has been overcome in:

## THE SIMPLIFIED COUNT

Here, all counters are simply valued at 10 each, using only those in the higher brackets.

The values run:

| | |
|---|---|
| Each ACE counts | 10 Points |
| Each TEN counts | 10 Points |
| Each KING counts | 10 Points |
| Total | 30 |
| Times 8 (of each type) | 240 |
| Plus LAST TRICK | 10 |
| TOTAL | 250 |

While this method obviously simplifies the count, it simplifies the play as well, which is why some Pinochle experts do not like it. With the "Original Count" a player must keep track of nearly every card, mentally calculating the odd totals as they increase during the play and possibly winning or losing a hand by a scant 2-point margin determined by the fall of a single Jack. That's real Pinochle.

Contrarily, the advocates of the "Simplified Count" argue that it speeds the game at every stage. A player can gauge the possibility of his hand more rapidly; the play itself is swift as minor values are eliminated; finally, the score can be totalled by a quick look through the tricks.

With this count, units may be used instead of tens. A player speaks of a hand being "worth 35" instead of "350." Counters themselves are simply valued as "1" instead of "10." For fast play, this certainly has advantages and except when the score is very close, the play requires about the same amount of skill.

To please both parties another type of count was introduced, namely:

## THE COMPROMISE COUNT

This retains much of the ease found in the "Simplified Count" and regains some of the flavor of the old "Original Count." Its values are:

| | |
|---|---|
| Each ACE counts | 10 Points |
| Each TEN counts | 10 Points |
| Each KING counts | 5 Points |
| Each QUEEN counts | 5 Points |
| Total | 30 Points |
| Times 8 (of each type) | 240 Points |
| Plus LAST TRICK | 10 |
| TOTAL | 250 |

Whether this compromise succeeds is another question. Perhaps the best method is to test it and even then, it depends upon the preference of the players themselves. In brief:

## THE BEST COUNT TO USE

is the one that best fits the occasion or pleases the participants in the game. The Original Count is traditional in Pinochle; therefore, to retain it in a good old-fashioned Two-Handed game seems logical indeed.

But by the same token, the Simplified Count becomes logical in Auction Pinochle, the most popular version of the game today, because Auction itself is a modern derivation, designed for fast action, with the play's importance frequently minimized.

However: Players familiar with one type of Count do not like to switch to the other, as it throws them off their game. When that becomes the bone of contention, the Compromise Count does supply an answer.

It penalizes both factions. Players familiar with the Original Count have to forget about the Jacks and give more emphasis to the King and Queen; while those who customarily use the Simplified Count must remember that the King's value is halved in the Compromise Count and must also consider the equal value of the Queen.

In the discussions that follow, the Simplified Count (A-10, 10-10, K-10) will be used unless otherwise specified, merely because it makes the totals easier to add and thereby requires less detail. Due consideration will be given to the other systems, however, particularly the Original Count, which some players still regard as the pinnacle of Pinochle.

# Chapter II

## MELD, DRAW AND PLAY

Once familiar with the Meld, the Count and the comparatively simple, though exacting Rules of Play, the beginner will know all he needs about Pinochle.

He won't have to worry whether the name is derived from "binocle" as in binoculars, or whether it was always "pinochle" as in pig's knuckles

It won't matter to him whether the game was first played immediately after the Battle of Hastings or just before the founding of Hastings-on-Hudson.

He won't care whether the Nine of Trumps is spelled "Deece" instead of "Dix" because French spelling is regarded as obsolete except by some 10,000,000 Americans living in the state of Illinois.

The Meld, itself, varies in different types of Pinochle and is restricted by the number of cards in the player's hand—something that is also a variable factor according to the game. In the previous chapter, a List of Melds was given, along with some comments on their restrictions and irregularities.

But it is not enough merely to tabulate such rules. Actual examples are needed, otherwise the Meld can cause confusion and dispute. So for perhaps the first time in a book on Pinochle, sample melds are illustrated in detail, not just to cover any problems that may rise, but to familiarize the reader with the actual Melds.

These examples refer to the games of Three-Handed and Four-Handed Pinochle, as played with the regulation 48 card pack. This includes the most popular of all such games, Auction Pinochle. In such games, the Rules of the Meld differ somewhat from those of Two-Handed Pinochle, which will be taken up in a separate description of the Two-Handed game.

It has already been stated that each Meld must be formed by the addition of a new card or cards. It is also required that each and every meld be complete in itself, though any card may figure in another meld of an entirely different type.

Take as the simplest example, an Ordinary Marriage, plus either the King or Queen of the same suit:

K♠ Q♠ K♠

This counts as a Marriage in Spades, giving the melder 20 Points (or 40 for a Royal Marriage in Trumps). The extra King can not be mated with the lone Queen to produce another Marriage. Bigamy is against the law in Pinochle.

As a similar case, a player may hold seven Jacks:

J♠   J♡   J♣   J◇   J♠   J♡   J♣

But only four can figure as Forty Jacks (40 Points) because such a combination must be complete in itself. The same applies to melds of four Queens, Kings and Aces.

Here, however, is a case where a single card can figure not just in two Melds, but in *three*, since each is of a different type:

```
                                    K♠
                            Q♠
        A◇  10◇  K◇  Q◇   J◇
                            J♣
                            J♡
                            J♠
```

The "three-way" card is the Jack of Diamonds. It is part of a Trump Sequence (150 Points) and a member of a Forty Jacks combination (40 Points) and it also teams with the Queen of Spades to form a Pinochle (40 Points). By adding the King of Spades to the Queen, we also have a Marriage (20 Points) making the total 250 Points.

Note that the Sequence shown above includes a King and Queen of Diamonds. Since they are part of the Trump Run, they can not be counted as a Royal Marriage.(*) They are simply members of the Sequence, contributing to its value of 150 Points.

While this looks rather obvious in most cases, it can produce complications in the following:

```
        A♡  10♡  K♡  Q♡  J♡
            K♠    K◇    K♣
            Q♠    Q◇    Q♣
```

Here are two strong Melds, a Trump Sequence in Hearts (150) and a Round Trip (240). But both can not be scored together for a desired total of 390.

The reason: A Round Trip is composed of Four Marriages, each in a different suit. But the King and Queen of Hearts are not counted as a Marriage and can not be, unless the Sequence is sacrificed.

―――――
*At times this is permissible in Two-Handed Pinochle where the melding is progressive as will be explained in the chapter on that game.

But it's not so bad as it looks. You don't have to drop 150 Points to score the 240. All you lose is 40 for the Royal Marriage which is sacrificed. The Meld would be formed thus:

Start with the Sequence, counting ...............150
Add the three extra Kings, counting ............ 80
Add the Queen of Clubs (as a Marriage) .... 20
Add the Queen of Diamonds (a Marriage) 20
Add the Queen of Spades (a Marriage) ........ 20
Link these three Queens with the
    Queen of Hearts(*) as added card .... 60

                TOTAL ...........................350

This pretty well clarifies the subject of Melds, but another example will prove helpful, particularly because it answers another often-echoed question: "What is the largest Meld a player can lay down from one hand?"

In Auction Pinochle, a three-handed game commonly played with a Widow, each player is dealt 15 cards (leaving three over for the "Widow" as the extra cards are called). Obviously, the Meld must be limited to 15 cards—which in itself is something remarkable!—but even then, the possible combinations will vary in their playing values.

Here is about the highest possible Meld with a 15-card hand:

| A ◇ | 10 ◇ | K ◇ | Q ◇ | J ◇ | 9 ◇ |
| A ♠ |      | K ♠ | Q ♠ |     |     |
| A ♡ |      | K ♡ | Q ♡ |     |     |
| A ♣ |      | K ♣ | Q ♣ |     |     |

This hand totals up as follows:

TRUMP SEQUENCE (in Diamonds) ....150
FOUR ACES (HUNDRED ACES) ........100
FOUR KINGS (EIGHTY KINGS) ........ 80
FOUR QUEENS (SIXTY QUEENS) .... 60
PINOCHLE (JD and QS) ......................... 40
MARRIAGE in Spades ............................. 20
MARRIAGE in Hearts ............................. 20
MARRIAGE in Clubs ............................... 20
DIX (9 of Trump) ..................................... 10

           TOTAL POINTS ............500

---

*In Three- and Four-Handed Pinochle, a card may be "added" when already in a Meld. But in Two-Handed, one must be added from the hand, as will be seen.

From the standpoint of play, however, this is not the strongest hand that a player can hold in Auction Pinochle. It contains too many losing cards where taking tricks is concerned. In the play, this hand might not take more than 80 or 90 points out of a possible 250 though there are factors that could improve that score.

Granting that it should make 600 (that is, 500 Meld + 100 Play) can this hand be bettered? The answer is definitely, yes. Most experts agree that the nearest to a "perfect" Pinochle hand is this one:

| A ◇ | 10 ◇ | K ◇ | Q ◇ | J ◇ |
|-----|------|-----|-----|-----|
| A ◇ | 10 ◇ | K ◇ | Q ◇ | J ◇ |
| A ♠ |      | Q ♠ | Q ♠ |     |
| A ♡ |      |     |     |     |
| A ♣ |      |     |     |     |

Here, it will be noted, the player has a "Double Run" or two Sequences in the Trump suit. So the hand adds up:

TRUMP  SEQUENCE ..................................150

2ND TRUMP SEQUENCE .........................150

HUNDRED ACES .......................................100

DOUBLE PINOCHLE .............................. 80

  TOTAL POINTS ...................................480

This is only 20 points less than the previous hand but the playing potential is much greater, in fact so much greater, that right here we shall introduce the reader to some essential features in the play of a Pinochle hand.

In this hand, the player would lead with the Ace of Trump, following with the other Ace of Trump if needed, in order to clear out the two missing Nines of Trump held by the other players.

He would do this, rather than risk any of his "bare" Aces (Hearts or Clubs), or even the Ace of Spades. The reason: One opponent might be "blank" in the suit led and would therefore trump it. Then, by leading back other Aces, the opponent might capture one or both of our player's "bare" pair.

The opponents aren't likely to "have it so good," but there's a slim chance that they might. So with such powerful Trumps in his hand, our player should first "clear" the Trump Suit. He would then follow with the various Aces and more Trumps, thus winnowing down the other hands.

But before playing either of his "losers"—the Queens of Spades—he should reserve enough Trump cards to make sure of taking "Last Trick" which counts for 10 points. Normally, he would need to hold two Trumps to be sure of this, because his opponents know exactly what he holds, having seen his entire hand melded on the board.

By all rights, our player should lose just two tricks, those Queens which he melded because they gave him 40 Points each, through their affinity for the Diamond Jacks. Now our question is: How many points will the Queens cause our player to lose?

Pinochle players, being pessimists, will say "20 Points each." The calculation is simple. Our player leads a Queen of Spades and one opponent puts on a King of Spades and the other a Ten of Spades.

When the second Queen of Spades is played, the opponents hit it with another pair of "counters"—say the Ace and King. So in all, they have deprived our player of 40 Points. This means he is "sure" of 210, provided he plays his hand intelligently, which is simple in this instance.

So the hand shown above rates at a minimum of 690 Points (480 + 210) according to conservative estimates. You can't do worse, but can you do better?

Very easily, if the breaks happen to be with you. Sometimes it is impossible for the opponents to make the few points that they might, simply because the cards happen to be against them.

In Auction Pinochle, the successful bidder has the privilege of picking up a three-card "Widow" and discarding three other cards in its stead. The Widow can be highly helpful, as we shall see as we proceed. For one thing, the discard becomes part of the player's score.

Now, suppose in this instance that the bidder's "super" hand (as exhibited above) also contained the second Ace of Spades and the two Tens. What a "super-super" hand he would then hold! He would have to discard three cards that would be sure trick winners in order to cash in his 80 Points for Double Pinochle!

It would be worth discarding those winners, however, as they are all "counters" and would therefore mark up 30 points to the bidder's credit when he put them away. But equally important, those Spade counters would no longer be out against our player, the bidder.

We had him figured to lose 40 Points, namely 20 with each Queen of Spades he played. But he can't lose 40 Points if his opponents follow suit. He can only lose 20 Points because there are only two counters—the Kings—still out against him.

And if he gets a nice break, he will only lose 10 Points. To prove this, let's suppose that the hands are as follows:

*Bidder:*

| A♦ | 10♦ | K♦ | Q♦ | J♦ | |
| A♦ | 10♦ | K♦ | Q♦ | J♦ | |
| A♠ | | Q♠ | Q♠ | | |
| A♡ | | | | | |
| A♣ | | | | | |
| | *Discard:* | A♠ | 10♠ | 10♠ | |

*Opponent A:*

| K♠ | J♠ | J♠ | 9♠ | 9♠ | |
| A♡ | 10♡ | 10♡ | Q♡ | 9♡ | 9♡ |
| K♣ | K♣ | Q♣ | 9♣ | 9♣ | |

*Opponent B:*

| 9♦ | 9♦ | | | | |
| K♠ | K♠ | | | | |
| K♡ | K♡ | Q♡ | J♡ | J♡ | |
| A♣ | 10♣ | 10♣ | Q♣ | J♣ | J♣ |

Here's what can then happen.

Suppose the Bidder is in a daring mood. He leads the Ace of Hearts and then the Ace of Clubs, picking up a trick with each. Next, he leads the Ace of Spades and captures a King, one of the two counters against him, from Opponent B.

Figuring the lay of the cards, the bidder leads the Queen of Spades, which Opponent B takes with his other King. Now, whatever Opponent B may lead, the Bidder takes the next trick. The Bidder then leads his other Queen of Spades. Opponent A must throw an odd Spade—as he did before—and Opponent B must trump with a Nine of Diamonds, which has no "count" value.

From then on, the Bidder takes all the tricks and rings up a count of 240, giving him a total score of 720 (480 + 240) which represents the maximum that this hand can promise.

It's possible for him to score 250 if an opponent goes stupid, but hands should not be rated on that basis. The Bidder could go dumb, too, and throw away tricks himself. So all hands should be analyzed according to normal or intelligent play.

We still haven't come to the "perfect" Pinochle hand. You can't quite make it in a game of Auction with Widow, as 15 cards in the playing hand aren't quite enough. You find it in a regulation Three-Handed game in which each player is dealt 16 cards. Here it is:

| A♠ | 10♠ | K♠ | Q♠ | J♠ |
| A♠ | 10♠ | K♠ | Q♠ | J♠ |
| A♦ | A♦ | | | |
| A♣ | A♣ | | | |
| A♡ | A♡ | | | |

This adds up:

Double Trump Sequence ...............................300
Two Sets of Hundred Aces ...........................200
Total Points .................................................500

Lead off with Trumps and continue until they have all been used. Then play the six remaining cards—all Aces. The hand can't miss. It adds a score of 250 Points for a total of 750. Try and top that!

## GROUPS OF MELDS

### CLASS A

| | | | | | | |
|---|---|---|---|---|---|---|
| SEQUENCE | A♡ | 10♡ | K♡ | Q♡ | J♡ | 150 Points |
| ROYAL MARRIAGE (TRUMP) | K♡ | Q♡ | | | | 40 Points |
| SIMPLE MARRIAGE | K♠ | Q♠ | or K♣ | Q♣ | | |
| | | or K◇ | Q◇ | | | 20 Points |

### CLASS B

| | | | | | |
|---|---|---|---|---|---|
| HUNDRED ACES | A♡ | A♣ | A◇ | A♠ | 100 Points |
| EIGHTY KINGS | K♡ | K♣ | K◇ | K♠ | 80 Points |
| SIXTY QUEENS | Q♡ | Q♣ | Q◇ | Q♠ | 60 Points |
| FORTY JACKS | J♡ | J♣ | J◇ | J♠ | 40 Points |

### CLASS C

| | | | | | |
|---|---|---|---|---|---|
| PINOCHLE | | J◇ | | Q♠ | 40 Points |
| DOUBLE PINOCHLE | J◇ | J◇ | Q♠ | Q♠ | 80 Points |

### CLASS D

| | | | |
|---|---|---|---|
| DIX (Pronounced "Deece") | 9♡ | (Trump) | 10 Points |

### SPECIAL

| | | | | | |
|---|---|---|---|---|---|
| ROUND HOUSE | K♡ | K♣ | K◇ | K♠ | 240 Points |
| (Or ROUND TRIP) | Q♡ | Q♣ | Q◇ | Q♠ | |

*Note*: Cards used in Melds of Class A, B or C can also be used in Melds that fall in other classes.

## Chapter III

## AUCTION PINOCHLE

So far, the subject of Pinochle has been discussed in a general way, with emphasis on the matters of the deck, the meld and the points, rather than the details of the play. This, the reader will have gathered, is due to the fact that Pinochle itself has many variations.

The most important of these from the standpoint of the modern Pinochle player is the game technically styled "Auction with a Widow" or simply "Auction" for short. For that reason, most of the comments and hints on play—as so far given—have been related chiefly to Auction Pinochle. But the full details have been reserved until this chapter for good and sufficient reasons, namely:

Aside from Auction being a comparative newcomer in the Pinochle family, the game of Auction itself is subject to variations, some in play but more particularly in scoring. So a step by step discussion of the game is the only way to clarify those details.

### NUMBER OF PLAYERS

Auction Pinochle is essentially a 3-player game, so far as the play of each hand is concerned, but 4 or even 5 persons may participate. In many circles, the 4-player game is preferred, as the dealer "sits out" each hand and therefore has no chance to manipulate the pack to his own advantage.

In the 5-player game, the dealer skips the person immediately to his left and starts the deal with the next player, continuing around the table, but eliminating himself as well.

With only three players, the dealer naturally includes himself. After each hand, the deal goes to the player on the left. Each player's object is to win each hand in which he participates by as high a score as possible.

### DEALING THE CARDS

Players cut the pack to see who deals and here we come to the first option. Some authorities claim that "low card" deals, as is customary in many other games. Others say that "high card deals."

Though it doesn't particularly matter, our preference is "high card" as a Pinochle pack is composed exclusively of high cards (Nines and

17

above) and it seems a trifle absurd to "go for low" in a pack that lacks such familiar cards as Deuces and Treys.

As to the deal itself: Here, again variants arise. Two processes are common.

(A)  Deal 4 cards to each active player.
     Deal 3 cards as a Widow.
     Deal 4 cards to each player.
     Deal 4 cards to each player.
     Finish with 3 cards to each player.

This gives each player 15 cards. The other process is still simpler— and better, namely:

(B)  Deal 3 cards to each active player.
     Deal 3 cards to the Widow.
     Continue dealing 3 cards around the board until each player
          has 15 cards.

System "B" is preferable as there are less cards in most of the clusters. This distributes them more effectively and thereby lessens the chance of cheating in "big money" games. Actually, there is no absolute rule as to how the cards should be dealt, but one thing is imperative:

*Never allow the three Widow cards to be dealt last.*

The Widow is actually a "bonus" for which players "bid" with the prospect of "improving" their hands. Any player who glimpses one or more of the Widow cards, whether accidentally or intentionally, gains an unfair advantage. Bottom cards are more apt to be exposed during the course of a deal than those in other portions of the pack.

## BIDDING THE HANDS

Once the cards have been dealt, each player proceeds to "bid" his hand. The bid starts with the player on the dealer's left and continues around the circle. Each player must either pass or bid. Once he passes, he can not bid again, but must pass automatically. After two players have passed, a bid stands.

For example: The first player bids 250. The second player passes. The third player "ups" the bid to 300. The first player raises it to 310. The second player must pass. The third player goes 320. Now, the first player passes. Since the second player is already "out" the auction goes to the third player.

Note here: The difference between a simple "bidding" card game and an "auction" game is that there is no restriction on the number of bids in Auction. In the original bidding games (from which Auction

Pinochle is partially derived) there was only one bid allowable to a player. The auction idea, of players bidding one another higher, has added zest to the game.

Yet, peculiarly, a single bid is often all a competent Pinochle player needs. Having properly evaluated his hand, he should know what it is worth. To underbid may prove as costly in the long run as to overbid. These are fine points, however, that will be discussed later. For the present, confining ourselves to the bidding process alone, we find that:

In many games, a minimum bid is set, sometimes as low as 1500, but usually 2000 and more often 2500. Whoever opens the bidding must go that amount or more. If all three players pass, the cards are tossed in and the deal moves on to the next player. However, various other rulings are frequently employed, such as:

(a) The player at the dealer's left may be required to open the bidding with 250, or better.

(b) The first two players may pass, but the third man must open for 250 or better.

(c) With a 250 minimum, the first two players may pass, but the third player must bid either 290 or make a bid higher than 300.

All these are optional rules which will be discussed in further detail later, along with other factors in the bid. Most important is that whoever wins the bid is stuck with it—unless he has the foresight to stay within the limitations of his hand and the possibilities of the Widow.

When two players have passed, following a bid, the Widow is turned up for all to see. The person who "won" the bid adds the three Widow cards to his hand. He then decides upon his Trump and melds. Here, again, certain optional rules may be introduced, as will be specified in due course.

While his Meld is on the table, where everyone else can count it too, the bidder must discard three cards from his hand. He may change his discard or his Meld and he may switch to another Trump if he so desires, provided this is done before the first trick is played. But always the discard should be made while the final Meld is still in view.

Otherwise, the bidder might discard some of the cards that he has melded, which is not permissible. The reason is that the discard goes with the tricks that the bidder takes. So if he places "counters" in the discard, he is that many points ahead before the play begins.

For example: Suppose that the bidder has a Ten, a King, two Jacks and two Nines that he has not used in the Meld. Assuming that the Ten and King are in a weak Suit and unlikely to win a trick, he should discard them in order to get the benefit of their count.

Now, if the bidder could pick up a King and Queen that he had melded and add the King to his discard, he would be picking up 10 points by the Simplified Count. To prevent this, the final Meld should be on the board until after the discard and the first play.

In fact, most experienced Pinochle players begin by leading the first card while the Meld is still on display. Since Pinochle rules are optional; that is, dependent upon the agreement of all the players, this is one rule that should belong in the game, by unanimous insistence. If the dealer opens play while his Meld is still up and his discard down, there can be no argument.

Any other player may demand to see the final Meld before play begins, so a lot of time can be saved by adhering to the practice of leading the first card—either from the hand or the Meld—while the Meld is still on display. It's fair, above-board and so far preferable to any monkey business of picking up the Meld before discarding that it is hard to see how competent Pinochle players could tolerate any dubious procedure.

Let the bidder discard with the Meld still on the board; then lead either before or after picking up the Meld. But always, the discard should be "buried" before the lead, because it is to the bidder's own advantage.

The reason: The bidder does not have to show his discard. Often he can "bury" cards which his opponents do not realize that he holds, thus giving himself a slight advantage in the play, where a slight advantage may prove tremendous. It would be almost idiotic to sacrifice this edge by mishandling the Widow, thus causing the opponents to insist that the hand be called void.

That is, unless the bidder had some ulterior motive, such as trying to get away with an illegal discard. That isn't good Pinochle, nor good sense, when a man's opponents outnumber him two to one—or more. Besides, it spoils the game. A lot of night watchmen may play Pinochle, but Pinochle enthusiasts don't like playing watchman during a night session of their favorite game.

A bidder may bury cards that he might have used in a Meld without mentioning that fact. He may also discard a Trump if he desires, but it has become an almost accepted rule that he must state that he has buried a Trump card (or cards) though he does not have to name its value.

When this amateurish procedure crept into vogue, and how, is hardly a matter of consequence. Suffice it that the "ruling" should be ignored in any Pinochle party worthy of the name. The notion not only lacks authority; it violates fundamental Pinochle practice.

The bidder is counting on *all* he can get from the Widow. What's more, he's entitled to it. That's not only basic, it's logical, since he usually has to overbid his hand to get those cards, in order to obtain them. Every possible advantage should accrue to the successful bidder, where the Widow is concerned, because the whole idea of Auction is to force the bidding to go beyond its proper bounds.

If a player studies his hand and finds that he might cleverly nail a few more points in play by secretly discarding a Trump card, why should he be penalized for that foresight? The one answer is: He shouldn't be. Such a ruling lops off one of Pinochle's most golden chances.

Besides, the declaration of a discarded Trump is doubly self-contradictory. First: The act of discarding is essentially a secret process, so if a player has to declare that he discarded a Trump, the process has become open. Second: Since it has become open, the bidder should have to show the Trump in question, rather than practically say "Guess which" to the opponents.

If they have to guess, they may suggest that the bidder didn't bury a Trump at all. If he had been suspected of such chicanery in the past, they could demand proof or else refuse to play the hand. That would mean the bidder would have to show the discarded Trump anyway.

Carried further, he would have to show *all* the cards he buried after *every* successful bid, to prove that no Trumps were among them. Summed, the so-called "rule" not only contradicts but defeats itself. Such "guessing games" come under the head of Old Maid, not Pinochle.

Our guess is that it came into vogue during the period when Auction Pinochle was emerging from a strange limbo during which many players misconstrued certain rules and formed their own interpretations, often a confusion of one procedure with another. All such questionable variations should be banned from smart Pinochle—and all Pinochle should be smart.

As an example of a Bid, Meld and Discard, let's take the following hand:

| A♣ | K♣ | K♣ | Q♣ | Q♣ | J♣ | J♣ | 9♣ |
|----|----|----|----|----|----|----|----|
| 10♢ | K♢ | Q♢ | J♢ | | | | |
| K♡ | Q♡ | | | | | | |
| J♠ | | | | | | | |

This hand has big possibilities if the bidder can "connect" from the Widow. It's the sort of hand that might be overbid, so we will presume that he went as high as 350 and was very lucky to pick up the Widow and find:

K♢     Q♠     J♡

These add greatly toward the Meld but not toward playing strength. The bidder needs all he can get from the Meld which he displays as follows:

| K♣ | Q♣ | K♣ | Q♣ | J♣ | 9♣ |
|----|----|----|----|----|----|
|    |    | K♦ | Q♦ | J♦ |    |
|    |    |    | Q♠ | J♠ |    |
|    |    | K♡ | Q♡ | J♡ |    |

This Meld adds up:

| | |
|---|---|
| Two Royal Marriages (Clubs) | 80 |
| Sixty Queens | 60 |
| Forty Jacks | 40 |
| Pinochle (J D and Q S) | 40 |
| Marriage (Diamonds) | 20 |
| Marriage (Hearts) | 20 |
| Nine of Trump | 10 |
| TOTAL TRUMP | 270 |

The cards still in the bidder's hand consist of:

A♣  J♣  10♦  K♦

Unless he wishes to sacrifice some item of the Meld (such as the 20 points of the Diamond Marriage) he must make the discard from those cards he holds in hand. Assuming that he does this, he would bury the following:

10♦  K♦  J♣

This would give him two "counters"—the Ten and King of Diamonds—already toward his score from tricks. It would also bury a Trump leaving him one short in the play. Why he should have to say so is not only a mystery; it isn't Pinochle. Some players might break up a Meld rather than declare a buried Trump and no game should include rules that force such false issues.

We come now to the play of the hand:

The bidder starts by leading any card he wants. Years ago, there was an optional rule that the bidder must lead a Trump, some circles even insisting that it be his highest Trump. This is probably what began the silly business of announcing that a trump had been buried with the discard, since if the bidder buried his highest Trump, he obviously couldn't lead it.

But in sound Auction, the Trump lead was never demanded. The bidder, as stated, may lead whatever he wants and the other players are compelled to follow suit if they can. They may play any card of the Suit that they wish and the highest takes the trick, unless:

A player is out of the Suit led, in which case, he must play a Trump, if he has one, and the Trump takes the trick. Should two players be out of the Suit led, both must play Trumps, if they have them. This is known as "forcing out" Trumps.

If a player can not follow suit or play a Trump, he throws on an odd card of some other suit. Since this goes to the winner of the trick, it is customary for one player to "throw" a "counter" to another, when both are playing against the bidder. This, in pinochle parlance, is termed a "schmeer."

When a Trump is led, each succeeding player *must* play a *higher* Trump if he has it. This system of "forcing out" the higher Trumps has a great bearing on Pinochle play and is therefore an important rule. It applies *only* when Trumps are led, though in the early days of Auction, this rule too had variations, sometimes being applied when odd suits were trumped.

The bidder places the tricks he takes with the discarded Widow, while the other two players, combining their efforts to beat him, place their tricks in a mutual pool. The points are then counted and the bidder adds his to the total of his Meld.

If the grand total equals the amount of his bid, or better, he wins the exact amount of the bid from his opponents, but no more. That is, if he bids 360, he gets credited with that score, no matter how many extra points he may pile up. If he fails to make the bid, he loses double that amount to each of the other players.

As stated earlier, points gained in play may be calculated by different systems. To show how close these are apt to come, we shall cite an actual play of the hand described earlier in this chapter. The bidder won seven tricks, which with the discards gave him 24 cards that included:

2 Aces—3 Tens—4 Kings—4 Queens—5 Jacks.
By the *Original Count*, this would score:
Aces, 22; Tens, 30; Kings, 16; Queens, 12; Jacks, 10.
This, plus Last Trick (10) would total 100.

Using the *Simplified Count* it would add to:
Aces, 20; Tens, 30; Kings, 40; Last Trick, 10. This would produce exactly the same total of 100.

By the *Compromise Count*, the score would run:
Aces, 20; Tens, 30; Kings, 20; Queens, 20. Adding 10 for the Last Trick, this also totals 100.

This seldom works out so exactly, however. In another test of the same hand (against different arrangements in those of the opponents) the bidder racked up these totals:

Original Count ............................................................106

Simplified Count ........................................................ 90

Compromise Count ..................................................... 85

Even here, the results show only about 20 points variance. With a meld of 270, the bidder needs at least 80 points to make his 350 bid, so he manages to skim through on all counts. That brings us to the objective of Auction Pinochle, namely:

The bidder, if he attains his bid, wins a specified number of chips or other tokens from the remaining players. Should he concede his hand as lost, without playing it, he must give that number of tokens to the other players.

Usually, these numbers are rated on the basis of a "chip a hundred." This starts at the minimum, say 250 and goes up from there. The bidding is further stimulated by jumping the stakes by fives, for example:

A score of 250 wins or loses 5 chips each.
A score of 260 wins or loses 5 chips each.
A score of 270 wins or loses 5 chips each.
A score of 280 wins or loses 5 chips each.
A score of 290 wins or loses 5 chips each.
A score of 300 wins or loses 10 chips each.
A score of 350 wins or loses 15 chips each.
A score of 400 wins or loses 20 chips each.

This continues on the same pattern: 450 is worth 25 chips; 500 rates at 30 chips. In brief, though each 100 means an added chip, the jumps come only at the end of each 50 points. Other scales of increase are sometimes used by agreement, especially in the higher brackets, as:

With a bid of 400, the stakes jump to 25 chips; with 450, to 35 chips; with 500 to 45 chips and so on. Players may use any increase scale that they please, the purpose being to encourage high or "longshot" bidding.

If the bidder plays out his hand, which he usually must do to prove that he can win it, he takes a double loss if he fails to make the bid.

Example: A player obtains the bid for 340. If he tosses in his hand, he pays the other 10 chips each, but if he plays and loses, he must pay them 20 each. If he makes the bid, he merely collects 10 from each.

Also: It is an almost universally accepted rule that when the bidder declares Spades as Trump, all stakes are doubled, win or lose. The "Double in Spades" rule is so widely recognized that it should be considered part of the game unless the players agree beforehand to forego it.

In recent years, the game has been "stepped up" further by having Hearts pay triple when named as Trump. This should be specified beforehand, as "Hearts Triple" is definitely an interloper. Some players would prefer to play for higher stakes rather than have certain hands "boosted" so far out of proportion.

An almost universal feature of modern Auction Pinochle is the Kitty. This is a pool to which players contribute or draw under certain circumstances. To begin, the players usually "ante" a specified number of chips into the kitty. Then:

When a player is forced to make a minimum bid (say 250 or 290 as earlier described) but feels that his hand is too poor to chance it, he can throw up the hand and pay the kitty a single chip instead of paying off the other players.

If a player does this, he must pay the kitty without looking at the Widow. In games where no minimum bid is required, all the players usually have to contribute to the kitty whenever every one passes.

In some games, the kitty collects just like the other players whenever the bidder tries to make a bid but fails. It does not collect if he concedes the hand, and if he wins his bid the kitty may—or may not—pay the bidder, according to how the players decide beforehand.

That applies whenever the bid is below a specified level, say 350. When the bid is 350 or higher, the kitty simply represents an additional player, paying or receiving just like the rest. This is the practice in all games where the kitty is used.

When the kitty becomes depleted, players must contribute chips to replenish it. Many other rules may be applied to the kitty, through mutual agreement on the part of the players. Since the kitty is their own pool, any player leaving the game is allowed to take his share and at the finish of the game itself, the pool is divided equally among the players.

Also, players may agree to incorporate certain bonus payments into the game itself, as giving a bidder one chip from each player if he melds a Hundred Aces without the aid of the Widow. Sometimes he may be given an extra chip for each 50 point level of his bid.

Such a bonus is paid only if the bidder wins his hand. The whole idea is to get him to bid on the strength of his Aces, particularly when payments increase at the graduated levels.

This covers the subject of how Auction Pinchole is played, with most of its ramifications. We come now to the part that readers already conversant with the game will most appreciate: How to play it and win.

## THE THREE STYLES
## OF COUNTS
## USED IN PINOCHLE

| EACH | ORIGINAL | SIMPLIFIED | COMPROMISE |
|---|---|---|---|
| ACE | 11 | 10 | 10 |
| TEN | 10 | 10 | 10 |
| KING | 4 | 10 | 5 |
| QUEEN | 3 | 0 | 5 |
| JACK | 2 | 0 | 0 |
| NINE | 0 | 0 | 0 |
| TOTAL | 30 | 30 | 30 |
| (For all Counters) | 240 | 240 | 240 |
| LAST TRICK | 10 | 10 | 10 |
| GRAND TOTAL | 250 | 250 | 250 |

## Chapter IV

## HOW TO BID AND WIN

In Auction Pinochle, the player who makes sure, sound bids should fare well, if he remembers that a "sound bid" is one that represents the hand's real worth, not just a portion of it. Let's take a case of three players all making "sure" bets on the strength of what their hands actually show.

Suppose they are playing with a 300 minimum paying 5 chips; 350 paying 10; 400 paying 20; 450 paying 30 and so on. Also assume that they are playing with a kitty that functions with bids of 350 or higher.

The player who hesitates at 340 when his hand is actually worth 360 is not making a "sound" bid. With 340, he will collect a mere 10 chips, 5 from each opponent. Whereas, 360 will bring 20 from the other players (10 each) plus another 10 from the kitty, totalling 30, or three times as much.

This is why "safe" players so often wind up losers. They don't make the most of their cards. They go on winning hands but losing chips all night, because a failure to collect is the same as paying out. In such company, the "sound" bidder will be the sure winner over a long run.

Many Pinochle players insist there is no positive formula for a Sound Bid. They follow an antiquated, inefficient process of first adding up the Meld, then guessing at how many "counters" they will lose, deducting those from 250 and crediting the difference to themselves. Usually, they add 20 or 30 Points as sure to come from the Widow, though why, they don't really know.

Usually, they will say that they heard on some authority that the Widow will improve a hand by 20 or 30 Points, or they may claim that experienced Pinochle players figure it that way. Many of them do, and they figure wrong in a lot of cases. There are times when the Widow is a shoo-in at 30 Points and others, when it is worth exactly 000, which spells "Zero—cipher—naught." Or to you, "Nothing."

Consider this sample hand:

| | | | | | |
|---|---|---|---|---|---|
| A ◇ | 10 ◇ | K ◇ | Q ◇ | J ◇ | J ◇ |
| | | Q ♠ | Q ♠ | J ♠ | 9 ♠ |
| | 10 ♡ | K ♡ | | | |
| | | K ♣ | K ♣ | Q ♣ | |

The Meld totals 250, consisting of a Sequence in Diamonds (Trump) 150; Double Pinochle, 80; a Simple Marriage (in Clubs) 20. That much is plain. Now the old-line Pinochle player guesses and being a pessimist, he guesses poorly.

Using the Simplified Count, he now begins to add up "losers" by a simple, time-honored method; namely, he figures to lose 30 on every "counter" as a Ten or King and he figures he will drop 20 on each "non-counter," a Queen, Jack or Nine.

Even the pessimist will concede that he should "Make good" his three top Trumps, the Ace, Ten and King. So he classes the remaining cards as "losers" and adds them mentally, usually quitting when sure they have him licked. If he completes this losing count, he will find he has:

> Three counters on the losing Ten Spot ........ 30
> Three each on three losing Kings .................... 90
> Two each on four losing Queens .................... 80
> Two each on three losing Jacks .................... 60
> Two on the losing Nine Spot ........................ 20
>
> TOTAL of Losing Points ........................ 280

Wonder of wonders, he has tagged himself for 30 points more than can possibly be lost! Happily, he remembers that the Widow is good for "20 or 30 Points" so he grants it 30 and cuts his loss down to 250. Again in the world of realism, he recalls that he conceded himself the three top Trumps, so each being a counter, he is sure to make 30 points and possibly another 10 for Last Trick.

So he rates hand as a possible 290 (the Meld of 250 + a safe 40 in Play) and refuses to bid the required 300 minimum that might net him a quick profit when there is no competition.

This situation has been somewhat exaggerated, but justifiably so, as it shows the dilemma that confronts the average bidder when he attempts to evaluate a hand by what some experts style good card sense, when it is really poor mathematics. To figure what he can take, then won't take, then might take, is confusing indeed and puts the player out on the proverbial limb.

Now let's see how a hand should be analyzed by the Sound Bid System, which supplants stupidity with science. Pinochle, from bid through play, can be handled mathematically, with "card sense" a negligible quantity, though it will grieve some proud Pinochle players to learn this.

A bidder is out to *win* points, not *lose* them, so the Sound Bid System starts from that standpoint, providing the sure formula which many Pinochle players have regarded as impossible.

## THE SOUND BID SYSTEM

This starts with the *Playing Count,* as it can be summed in terms of "winning" counters while arranging the hand and also has an important bearing on what follows. The first thing to look for, are Aces and Tens, as these are potential trick takers.

Count each Ace as 10. Count Double Ace 25.*
Count each 10 as 5. Ten with Double Ace, 10.

It's that simple. The Aces are practically sure points; the Tens have about an even chance, through play or being "buried" in the discard. But the count does not stop there. We come now to an even bigger factor in winning tricks and counters: Suit Strength.

Suit Strength first requires Suit Length. Any Suit with more than four cards is a "Long Suit." Every one of those additional cards is a powerful point snatcher in Pinochle, rating at 20 Points each.

In the sample hand shown, the Ace is worth 10, the two Tens are worth 10, the two extra Diamonds are worth 40. That adds up to 60 as the Playing Count.

Next, the *Meld Count.* The total of the Meld usually depends upon first naming a Trump. Only a Long Suit is satisfactory as Trump, which is why the Suits should be studied first. Having picked a Trump, the player adds his hand accordingly.

In this case, the only possible Trump is Diamonds. The Meld (as stated earlier) includes a Trump Sequence, a Double Pinochle, a Simple Marriage: $150 + 80 + 20 = 250$.

Finally, the *Widow Count.* The rule here is that whenever a card from the Widow helps a hand, it is necessary to make a discard. Therefore, the hand must first be studied in order to rate the Widow Value. On a conservative basis, add 10 Points for each card that can be discarded from the hand itself. You have then estimated the Widow Value (10, 20 or 30) automatically. Stop at 30 and also recognize 0 if the Widow can promise nothing.

The sample hand has three possible discards: The Ten of Hearts, King of Hearts, King of Clubs, all counters, with two non-counters, the Jack and Nine of Spades as reserves for discard. So the Widow Count is 30 Points.

This adds up:

|                     |        |
|---------------------|--------|
| Playing Count       | 60     |
| Meld Count          | 250    |
| Widow Count         | 30     |
| HAND VALUE          | 340    |

*This refers to two Aces in the same suit, as "Double Aces" in clubs.

That makes 300 a "Cinch Bid" and to stretch the bid 10 points to 350 should be safe enough, as with three counters all ready to be buried, and two extras in case the Kings can be melded, practically insures more than ordinary Widow help. To illustrate this, here are sample Widows dealt from the remaining cards.

| | | | |
|---|---|---|---|
| A♠ | K♦ | 9♡ | Ace adds 10 to Play; 20 to Suit. King, 20 to Suit. TOTAL 50. |
| A♡ | K♠ | Q♣ | Eighty Kings + Marriage. Add 100 Points. |
| 10♠ | 9♠ | 9♣ | Ten adds 5 to Play; 20 to Suit. Nine adds 20 to Suit. TOTAL 45. |
| A♠ | Q♦ | J♣ | Ace adds 10 to Play; 20 to Suit. Queen, 20 to Suit. TOTAL 50. |
| A♦ | A♣ | J♠ | Ace adds 10 to Play; 20 to Suit. Ace, 10 to Play; Jack, 20 to Suit. TOTAL 60. |
| A♣ | 10♣ | 9♡ | Ace adds 10 to Play; Ten, 5 to Play, 20 to Suit. TOTAL 35. |
| K♠ | J♣ | |J♡ | Eighty Kings + 20 added to Suit. TOTAL 100. |
| A♡ | K♡ | Q♡ | Ace adds 10 to Play; King & Queen, 20 Marriage. Queen, 60 Queens. TOTAL 90. |
| 10♦ | 9♦ | 9♣ | Ten, 5 to Play; 20 to Suit. Nine, 10 as Trump, 20 to Suit. TOTAL 55. |
| 10♣ | J♡ | 9♦ | Ten, 5 to Play; Nine, 10 as Trump; 20 to Suit. TOTAL 35. |
| 10♠ | 10♡ | Q♡ | Ten, 5 to Play; 20 to Suit; Ten, 5 to Play. Queen, 20 Marriage; 60 Queens. TOTAL 110. |

In a test play, with the weakest of these Widows and the remaining cards dealt into two hands quite favorable to the opponents, this hand made 100 Points, thus achieving the anticipated 350. The breakdown of counters ran:

|  | Original | Simplified | Compromise |
|---|---|---|---|
| Three Aces | 33 | 30 | 30 |
| Four Tens | 40 | 40 | 40 |
| Two Kings | 8 | 20 | 10 |
| Four Queens | 12 | — | 20 |
| Five Jacks | 10 | — | — |
| Last Trick | 10 | 10 | 10 |
| TOTAL COUNTS | 103 | 100 | 110 |

Here is another specimen hand which emphasizes the factor already mentioned regarding Widow Value; namely, that it should be determined on a sliding scale clear down to Zero, according to the player's ability to discard from his original hand:

A♣  A♣  K♣  K♣  Q♣  Q♣
K♡
K♠  Q♠  J♠  J♠  9♠  9♠
K♢  J♢

By the antiquated, unreliable "loser" count, a player can figure a dead loss on all but the four highest Clubs. By the Simplified Count, he'd give the opposition 90 Points on three non-trump Kings, 60 on three Queens, 60 on three Jacks, 40 on two Nines, for a total of 250.

Yet he has already figured on winning two Trump Aces (20) and two Trump Kings (20) with a hand good enough to nail Last Trick (10) so again the old "loser" style of calculation demonstrates its inefficiency.

The correct count on the Sound Bid System would run as follows:

*Playing Count:*

Double Aces, 25; Clubs Long Suit, 40; Spades Long Suit, 40. Total: $25 + 40 + 40 = 105$.

*Meld Count:* Double Marriage, Trumps, 80. Four Kings, 80. Pinochle, 40. Spade Marriage, 20. Total: $80 + 80 + 40 + 20 = 220$.

*Widow Value:* 0.

Here, the question of the Widow is most important. Its value, whether 0, 10, 20 or 30, is supposed to be the smallest help that it can possibly bring the hand. But with this hand, as we have rated it, the only help the Widow can supply is in the shape of "counters" that can be buried.

True there are 17 such counters (Aces, Tens, Kings) unaccounted for, but that means an average of less than 20 Points from ten possible Widows. This is not enough. It leaves every possible hand too scant.

An old-style "loser" count would give this hand about 270 Points, which is too small. The Sound Bid System gives it between 320 and 330, which is stretching it. The difficulty, however, lies in the lack of potential discards and that can be easily remedied.

Instead of dropping a weak Meld from the Count (which may be done to strengthen the hand) the proper move is to disregard Spades as a "Long Suit." This gives the hand four discards (Two Jacks and two Nines of Spades) which otherwise would be needed to maintain the Suit Strength.

That in turn deducts 40 Points from the Playing Count. But as compensation, it gives the hand a Widow Count of 30. So the bid adds up:

$$
\begin{aligned}
\text{Playing Count} &\dots\dots\dots\dots\quad 25 + 40 = 65 \\
\text{Meld} &\dots\dots\dots\quad 80 + 80 + 40 + 20 = 220 \\
\text{Widow Count} &\dots\dots\dots\dots\dots\dots\dots\quad\underline{30} \\
\text{TOTAL} &\dots\dots\dots\dots\dots\dots\dots\dots\quad 315
\end{aligned}
$$

Now for a series of Sample Widows, dealt from the remaining cards: The "test run" turned out as follows:

| | |
|---|---|
| A♡  Q♡  J♣ | Ace adds 10 in Play; Queen 20, Marriage; Jack, 20, Long Suit. TOTAL 50. |
| 10♡  Q♡  9♡ | Ten adds 10 (bury). Queen, 20, Marriage. TOTAL 30. |
| A♠  10♠  9♣ | Ace, 10 in Play. Ten, 10 (bury). Nine, 10 as Trump; 20 to Suit. TOTAL 40. |
| A♢  A♢  9♣ | Double Aces, 25 in Play; Nine, 10 as Dix of Trump; 20 to Suit. TOTAL 55. |
| A♡  10♢  10♣ | Ace, 10 in Play; Ten, 10 (bury). Ten, 10 in Play; 20 to Suit. TOTAL 50. |
| 10♠  K♢  J♣ | Ten, 10 (bury). King, 10 (bury). Jack, 20 to Suit. TOTAL: 40. |

| | | | |
|---|---|---|---|
| K♡ | Q♠ | J◇ | King, 10 (bury). Queen & Jack, Pinochle, 40. TOTAL: 50. |
| A♠ | J♡ | 9◇ | Ace, 10 in play. 40 (Spades becoming Long Suit). TOTAL 50. |
| K♠ | Q◇ | 9◇ | King, 10 (bury). Queen 20, Marriage. Gives Spades 20 for Long Suit. TOTAL: 50. |
| 10♣ | 10◇ | 10♡ | Ten of Clubs, 10 in Play; 20 to Suit. Bury others, 10 each. TOTAL: 50. |
| Q◇ | J♡ | 9♡ | Queen 20, Marriage. Give Spades 20 for Long Suit. TOTAL: 40. |

With the weakest of these Widows (the final one) and one opponent holding *all* remaining Spades, this hand still racked up 90+ Points in play, as follows:

| | Original | Simplified | Compromise |
|---|---|---|---|
| Three Aces | 33 | 30 | 30 |
| Two Tens | 20 | 20 | 20 |
| Three Kings | 12 | 30 | 15 |
| Five Queens | 15 | — | 25 |
| Five Jacks | 10 | — | — |
| Last Trick | 10 | 10 | 10 |
| TOTAL COUNT | 100 | 90 | 100 |

This would just make from 310 to 320 as estimated and in such cases, the lower total (310) should be used, so the bid was saved. However, the possibility of such a close shave brings up a very interesting factor.

This hand contained three Kings (non-trumps) which by the original calculation were due to be lost. Although we are reckoning hands by what they can *win*, it is obvious that the player will lose 10 Points (Simplified Count) on each of those Kings, though he wouldn't if the cards were Queens, or Jacks. Nor can any of those Kings be "buried" to save such loss because *all* figure in the Meld of Eighty Kings, which the bidder already added to the value of his hand.

Allowance can be made for this by following the simple rule:

After adding the value of the hand, deduct 10 Points for every Ten or King that can not be buried and may remain in the hand unguarded. A Ten is "unguarded" when holding less than three cards of its Suit. A King is "unguarded" when holding less than five of that Suit.*

---

*In some exceptional hands, as Double Ace over Double King, a King can often be "made good" in a 4-card Suit.

This deduction figures as an allowance only, simply adding that much to the security of the bid. For example: In the hand just analyzed, there are three "deductible" Kings, totalling 30 Points. This reduces the value of the hand from 315 to 285. But it would only require half of that "slack" or 30 point "allowance" to bid 300.

To show how allowance must sometimes be made for Tens, take the following freak hand as an example:

A◇    A◇    K◇    K◇    Q◇    Q◇    J◇    9◇    9◇
  10♠    10♠
  10♣    10♣
  10♡    10♡

This hand has a Meld of Double Royal Marriage, plus both Nines of Trump: 80 + 20 = 100. By the old "loser" count, the bidder will get clipped for 180 (losing 30 Points with each Ten) so he can count on a score of no more than 170.

By the Sound Bid System, the Double Ace is worth 25 and the six Tens rate 5 points each, a total of 55. To this is added 100 for five extra "Long Suit" cards at 20 each. This scores: 55 + 100 = 155.

Adding the Meld (100) this would come to 255, making the hand biddable with a 250 minimum. Widow value is 0 because three of those Tens *must* be buried to make the very 30 Points that the Widow is supposed to bring.

That still leaves three Tens unguarded, so another 30 Points should be deducted as "allowance" or "insurance" on the sound rule that they would lose 10 points less apiece if they were other cards than "counters." This means the hand is worth about 225, around 220 or 230.

It isn't biddable, but if the old "loser counter" won't believe the hand can make that much, it's not hard to show him. Absolutely anything can improve this hand.

The worst he can pick up would be three Nines in different suits. So he buries two Tens and a Nine of one Suit, say Spades. He can then trump that Suit as soon as it is led. The most he can lose will be 120 Points because that's all there are in Clubs and Hearts.

That gives him a sure 230 (100 + 130) and by leading a Ten to force an Ace, he is sure to make a Ten good in one Suit, and possibly a Ten in another, bringing his score up to 240 or 250. This shows how neatly and how closely the Sound Bid System can be figured. This hand, as shown, is worth a 250 bid. The 30 Point "leeway" is largely for worry warts or people who just won't believe it can be done.

It's like the story of the player who picked up his Pinochle hand and found he had a Double Sequence in Spades with three additional Aces, a sure 470, yet he never made it. The question was: How could he lose? The answer was, he didn't. He just dropped dead when he saw that he was holding such a hand.

The same applies to the Sound Bid system. We don't want customers dropping dead from the excitement of turning sure "losers" into "winners." They'd better take it slowly for a starter.

## THREE-HANDED PINOCHLE

The basic game from which Auction was derived.

Originally, each player was dealt 16 cards, the last card (to the dealer) being shown and its Suit declared to be Trump. Each player then shows his Meld and adds whatever Points he manages to take during the play. New hands are then dealt and the game continues. The player who first reaches 1000 is the winner.

In simple three-handed Auction, the Trump is not turned up. Instead, players bid and the highest bidder names the Trump. He makes his Meld and all the Points he can take; his opponents also Meld and score their Points.

The bidder's advantage, of course, is in the naming of the Trump, particularly if he has a Sequence or strong playing hand in that Suit. If he fails to make his bid, it is deducted from his score—and of course his Meld is lost with it. Object of the game is to reach 1000 Points.

In this game of 16-card hands, each player is on his own, but two often have to "gang up" on the third to keep him from going "out"—that is, from reaching 1000. It was this form of "partnership" that eventually developed the modern game of "Auction With a Widow" which is popularly styled "Auction" today, as the old scoring game is very little used.

There are other forms of "Three-Handed Pinochle" but none have even begun to gain the popularity of "Auction With a Widow" which is so fully discussed in this book.

## Chapter V

## BIDDING THE LIMIT

The player who adheres to the Sound Bid System has a solid basis on which to work and should be a consistent winner in ultra-conservative games as well as with erratic or highly headstrong bidders. That is, the Sound Bid System offers a better than average gain with an insurance against losses.

But suppose the bidding goes higher than the Sound Bid limit, yet the other players win a majority of their hands, as they very well may? What happens to the player who limits his bids to a "sure" count? The answer is, he loses, because he never gets a chance to bid.

True, he collects when the other bidders lose; but he pays out when they win. If, as stipulated, they are winning most of their bids, they will be taking the lion's share of the profits. Whether through luck, the fall of the cards, smart play, or a rabbit's foot in the hip pocket, it won't matter. They still may win.

As an example: Suppose a player stretches his hands to 350 and wins three out of four that should have been bid in the 300 bracket. He will collect 90 chips on the three good hands and pay out 30 by throwing in the bad one.

His profit will still be 60 chips.

But if he played conservatively and won all four hands on a 300 - 340 bid, he would only pick up 40 chips.

So he would still be 20 chips out, if he played it safe.* But would he manage to get in those sure bids? Not if the other players were stretching their bids and getting the breaks with it. His only answer would be to outbid them at their own game.

Don't misunderstand this. The Sound Bid is still the right bid, particularly when it hits in higher brackets and always when it is showing profits. But when the bidding gets above that level, the keen player will jump his own bid, for two reasons:

One: He may force another player to forego a sure winning bid.

Two: He may force other bidders to go beyond their reasonable limits.

That propounds the query: What is a reasonable limit? For practical

37

purposes, a "Limit Bid" as it will be styled, is one that offers the bidder an even break.

That in itself may surprise many Pinochle players. They may wonder what good it is to go on breaking even. It is very good, when done systematically, because it either stifles the other bidders or forces them to go wild and suffer heavy losses. The Limit Bidder wins as a result. Going back to the bidder who won three out of four at 350: Suppose *you* made "Limit Bids" up to the 400 bracket and took two such bids, winning one, losing the other, thus breaking even. Also suppose that *he* took the other two at 400 and lost both because he bid wildly.

He would lose 60 chips each time, a total of 120. That would be equivalent of his losing *all four* of the 350 bids at 30 chips each.*

Such results can be obtained by:

## THE LIMIT BID SYSTEM

Any bid beyond the safe and sound category is dependent upon Widow prospects. If the hand has three spaces to be filled, all offering the same amount of points—or better—your chances of filling are about even.

Take this hand as an example:

|     | A ◇ | K ◇ | Q ◇ |     |     |
|-----|-----|-----|-----|-----|-----|
| A ♡ | 10 ♡ | K ♡ | Q ♡ | J ♡ | 9 ♡ |
|     |     |     | Q ♠ | J ♠ | 9 ♠ |
|     |     | K ♣ |     | J ♣ | 9 ♣ |

There are three cards that can "fill" this hand for at least 80 Points. Already, it has a Meld of 160 in Hearts, plus 20 for a Marriage in Diamonds. But the needed cards for 80 Points improvement or better, are as follows:

K ♠ — This produces Eighty Kings and a Spade Marriage. Total: 80 + 20 = 100.

Q ♣ — This combines Sixty Queens with a Club Marriage. Total: 60 + 20 = 80.

J ◇ — This card goes with the Queen of Spades to form a Pinochle and also fills Forty Jacks. Total: 40 + 40 = 80.

*Refer back to previous chapter for the scoring system used.

In this case, the bid can be boosted 80 Points, because that represents the lowest of three possible "fills." The whole addition is:

| SOUND BID: | Playing Count: | 25 | (Aces and Ten) |
|---|---|---|---|
| | | 40 | (Long Trump) |
| | Meld Count: | 150 | (Sequence) |
| | | 20 | (Marriage) |
| | | 10 | (Dix) |
| | Widow Count: | 30 | |
| | SOUND BID: | 275 | |
| | Plus Potential: | 80 | |
| | LIMIT BID: | 355 | |

Here, a hand that couldn't make the 300 Minimum as a Sound Bid, becomes a Limit Bid of 350. There are five cards that can be buried: King, Jack, Nine of Clubs; Jack and Nine of Spades—except for those that may be required in "filling" the hand.

Other factors may enter in adding the potential value of the hand, when seeking help from the Widow toward a Limit Bid. Consider this hand:

| A♣ | K♣ | Q♣ | J♣ | 9♣ |
|---|---|---|---|---|
| A♡ | 10♡ | Q♡ | | |
| | 10♠ | Q♠ | Q♠ | |
| A♢ | K♢ | J♢ | J♢ | |

| SOUND BID: | Playing Count: | 40 | (Aces & Tens) |
|---|---|---|---|
| | | 20 | (Long Trump) |
| | Meld Count: | 40 | (Royal Marriage) |
| | | 80 | (Double Pinochle) |
| | | 10 | (Dix) |
| | Widow Count: | 30 | |
| | SOUND BID: | 220 | |

The Widow Count is justified by four expendable cards, the Tens of Hearts and Spades, the King of Diamonds and the Queen of Hearts, as the hand now stands. Naturally, any of these can be retained by simply burying odd cards from the Widow. So they can be figured in our calculations of possibilities:

10♣

This card will complete a Royal Sequence (150) adding 5 to Playing Value and 20 for added Suit Length. 150 + 5 + 20 = 175. But the Royal Marriage is absorbed, deducting 40. (175 — 40 = 135).

POTENTIAL
VALUE . . . . 135

A ♠

POTENTIAL
VALUE .... 120

This card completes 100 Aces
(100) and adds 10 to Playing
Value, with Four Aces in a hand,
a bonus of 10 is justifiable. (100
+ 10 = 120.)

Q ◇

POTENTIAL
VALUE .... 100

This card completes 60 Queens
(60) and a Marriage (20). It
also produces a Long Suit (20).
(60 + 20 + 20 = 100.)

This raises the Limit Bid on this hand from 220 to 320, represented
by the lowest of the three possible "fills." Note, however, that the
Queen was worth an extra 20 on Suit Length. These factors must be
noted in determining the lowest "fill" card. The higher cards do not
matter with the Limit Bid, since they have an additional margin. However, it is best to check them.

Mathematically, the odds are slightly against filling a Limit Bid.
Actually, the player's chances are better than even, due to a chance
bonanza from the Widow.

Here are three samples that turned up in a test deal:

K ♡
K ♠
9 ◇
ADDED VALUE .... 120

These two Kings, though a long
shot, would bring 80 Kings, plus
two Marriages at 20 each.
(80 + 20 + 20 = 120)

A ♣
A ♡
10 ◇

ADDED VALUE .... 100

The Aces are worth 15 each in
play, 20 each in Suit Length, with
a bonus of 10. The Ten (under
Double Ace) rates 10 in play,
20 in Suit. (15 + 15 + 20 + 20
+ 10 + 10 + 10 = 100)

K ♣
Q ♣
K ◇

ADDED VALUE .... 100

A Royal Marriage (40) adds two
cards to Long Suit (40) and the
King of Diamonds adds 20 to its
Suit.
(40 + 20 + 20 + 20 = 100)

While such freak "buys" seldom occur, they are helpful when they
do, so the bidder should not stretch his Limit Bid to its full extent unless
forced to do so. Suppose he started the bidding at 300 with the hand just
shown and was lucky enough to pick up:

J♣
K♠
K♠

ADDED VALUE .... 80

The Jack would give him 20 for
Suit and the two Kings would
bring 40 for two Marriages, with
20 more for Suit Length.

(20 + 20 + 20 + 20 = 80)

This improvement would make the hand playable on the basis of a
300 bid as determined by the original count. All such factors favor
the Limit Bid System. Some hands may show a *fourth* opening that
can be filled. These, too, help boost the player's chances to "better than
average" when using the Limit Bid System.

There is no use looking for "four spot" hands, however, nor is there
any good in rating them as a breed of their own. A hand so full of
"holes" seldom has enough of a Meld to make it even biddable. When
it does show a good Meld, the "fourth best" spot suffers accordingly,
usually being something like a "possible" Forty Jacks.

So such hands should be pooled with the regular "three chance" hands
that form the basis for the Limit Bid. They will help in the long run,
when the bidder doesn't have to stretch much beyond the fourth best
filler, which often gets some extra help from an odd card in the Widow.

Always rate the playing possibilities of the hand *after* picking up the
Widow and making the discard. Suppose you made a freak fill for 100
with the King of Clubs, Queen of Clubs and King of Diamonds. Your
discards would necessarily be the Ten of Spades, Ten of Hearts and
Queen of Hearts, giving you 20 "buried" Points.

Here's how your hand would then stand for the play to follow:

| A♣ | K♣ | K♣ | Q♣ | Q♣ | J♣ | 9♣ |
|----|----|----|----|----|----|----|

A♡

| Q♠ | Q♠ |
|----|----|

| A♢ | K♢ | K♢ | J♢ | J♢ |
|----|----|----|----|----|

We rate it thus:

| | | |
|---|---|---|
| Playing Count: | 30 | (Three Aces) |
| Long Suits: | 60 | (Clubs) |
| | 20 | (Diamonds) |
| Meld Count: | 80 | (Two Royal Marriages |
| | 80 | (Double Pinochle) |
| | 10 | (Nine of Trumps) |
| TOTAL: | 280 | |
| Extra Points: | 20 | (Buried Tens) |
| *Total + Extra* | 300 | |

Again, anyone who counts "losers" may be amazed at this, figuring it's only sure of 70 or 80 in the play. It's another of those hands where you could lose more than the whole 250, the way some people figure.

But apply some common-sense and you will see how nicely it should work out.

With the usual "lay" of Trumps, this hand should easily be dominant, as it holds seven, with only five out against it. Only *three* of those Trumps are "counters" (Ace, Ten and Ten) which can be forced by the Queens or the Jack.

The player should make one King of Diamonds good and very possibly both. His opponents, not knowing he is "long" on Diamonds may "cash" their Ace and Tens quickly. The bidder's Kings of Diamonds then become sure trick-takers.

Various factors govern the play of the hand and they will be discussed in a later chapter. We can sum the present situation by stating that the 110 needed as a Playing Count is within normal reach, provided those "buried" points are included. For instance, in a test play in which the "breaks" were somewhat against the bidder, he managed to bag:

|  | Original Count | Simplified Count | Compromise Count |
|---|---|---|---|
| Four Aces | 44 | 40 | 40 |
| Two Tens | 20 | 20 | 20 |
| Five Kings | 20 | 50 | 25 |
| Four Queens | 12 | — | 20 |
| Six Jacks | 12 | — | — |
| Last Trick | 10 | 10 | 10 |
| TOTAL | 118 | 120 | 115 |

The "buried" points—23, Original Count; 20, Simplified Count; 25, Compromise Count, were needed to make 280. The reason is: They were the sort of "counters" that the bidder would have "picked up" if they had been in the hands of his opponents. In brief:

If you stash away two or three counters in the discard, you have "won" them, so to speak, before the play starts, so to count these "extras" would be to count them twice. Counters are "sure" when buried; that is all. In this hand, the bidder would be going beyond his limit to try for 300. The hand is worth 280, no more. Note, however, that this represented a "freak fill" which did not figure in the original bid.

It is never advisable to go beyond the playing limit. People who advise stretching it overlook one factor, namely: You are always taking something of a chance when you bid up to the hilt. A wrong lay of the cards,

a freak hand held by an opponent, some unforeseen slip in the play—
any of these may mean the loss of what might have been a "sure" hand.

This has been taken into consequence in our ratings, which are by
no means 100% certain. The bidder will lose occasional hands that he
should or might have made, even if he stays within bounds. But the
bidding system, as given here, enables him to make the most out of
the hands he does win, so it should more than compensate.

## WATCH OUT FOR FREAK HANDS

Be careful not to overbid a hand that has a high Meld but very poor playing possibilities. As an example:

| K◇ | Q◇ | J◇ | J◇ | 9◇ |
|----|----|----|----|----|
| K♠ | Q♠ | Q♠ | J♠ | |
| K♡ | Q♡ | J♡ | | |
| K♣ | Q♣ | J♣ | | |

Discards: 9♡    9♡    J♣

Meld:    240   Round Trip
          80   Double Pinochle
          40   Four Jacks
          10   Dix (Hearts)
         ————
Total    370

Yet this hand might not make a 400 bid! You can count on 10 or 20 points (due to Long Suit in Trump) but more are doubtful. If one opponent should hold both Aces, Tens and the odd King of Hearts, you could lose every trick. A hand that takes no tricks loses its Meld, so it is actually possible for a freak like this to miss on the "sure" count that it already shows!

44

## Chapter VI

## BIDDING BEYOND THE LIMIT

Two factors have been stressed in the preceding chapter: The Bidding Limit and the Playing Limit.

The Bidding Limit, as we have described it, represents the "chance" that a bidder can normally take in "upping" his bid. The Bidding Limit is what he expects to make, if the Widow gives him one of three necessary "fills" or improves his hand (by a freak fill or extra help) to the extent that he hoped.

The Playing Limit is the amount he feels sure his hand can make *after* the bid, *after* the Meld and *after* the discard; namely, when he is ready to play his hand or toss it in. That's why he shouldn't go beyond it.

But it is possible and sometimes feasible to go higher than a "Limit Bid" when the bidding itself is still on. But the moment a player bids with less than three prospects of filling his hand, he is entering the danger zone. Under ordinary circumstances, he should avoid:

### THE RISK BID

This is a bid with only two chances of making the required fill. It is best illustrated by a sample hand:

| | | | | | |
|---|---|---|---|---|---|
| A♣ | 10♣ | K♣ | K♣ | Q♣ | Q♣ |
| A♡ | 10♡ | | | | |
| 10♠ | K♠ | Q♠ | Q♠ | | |
| A♢ | J♢ | J♢ | | | |

This adds up to:

| | | |
|---|---|---|
| Playing Count: | 45 | (Aces & Tens) |
| | 40 | (Long Suit) |
| Meld Count: | 80 | (Trump Marriages) |
| | 80 | (Double Pinochle) |
| | 20 | (Spade Marriage) |
| Widow Count: | 20 | (Only two discards) |
| Sound Bid | 285 | |

Now, this hand has two "spaces" that can be filled: The Jack of Clubs will jump its value 110 Points (150 for Sequence less 40 already counted for one Royal Marriage) with another 20 Points for Suit Strength. Added to 285 this would total 415.

The Ace of Spades will bring 110 Points boost (100 for Four Aces, plus 10 Points play) and even with the Ten of Spades discarded, there would be an added Suit Strength of possibly 20 Points.

With either fill, it would be a nice 400 bid, or even 410, except that it shouldn't be bid at all. And why not? Because the odds are just about 2 to 1 against filling the hand when only two spots are open.

Bid hands like these all night—like some players do—and you'll lose two bucks, chips or simoleons for every one you acquire—as some players also do. This raises the query: Why consider a "Risk Bid" at all?

Because there is a time to use it: When the game includes "Spades Double" and your Trump happens to be in Spades. In the hand just shown, suppose that the long Trump Suit happened to be Spades instead of Clubs. In that case, either "fill" would give the bidder a 400 hand in Spades.

In playing and winning such a hand, he would be paid double. If he didn't fill, he would simply toss in his hand without naming Trump and so pay off single. Since he has twice as much to win as lose, he is equalizing the bid. His "Risk Bid" in Spades, becomes the equivalent of a "Limit Bid" in another suit.

So it would be worth bidding, in a fast game where Limit Bids are in order. But the Risk Bid can be deceptive. Take this case:

| A♠ | 10♠ | K♠ | Q♠ | 9♠ |
| A♦ | K♦ | Q♦ | J♦ | 9♦ |
| A♣ | 10♣ | 10♣ | | |
| A♡ | 10♡ | | | |

With 60 Points for Playing Count (Aces & Tens) plus 40 for two Long Suits, a Hundred Aces (100), a sure Royal Marriage (40), with a Dix (10), plus an Ordinary Marriage (20), and a Pinochle (40) this hand is worth a Sound Bid of 340, since it has a Widow Value of 30 to go along with all the rest.

It's a natural temptation to bid it up to 480 on the chance of filling a Sequence with either the Jack of Spades or Ten of Diamonds. Here we have a Risk Bid and with Spades counting double, it should be worth it. Or would it?

It wouldn't. If you filled Spades, fine; but not if you filled Diamonds. Hands like these aren't 2 to 1 shots. They are only 1½ to 1. Double profits for Spades; only single profits for Diamonds.

That has represented a rule for good bidding this long while: Jump from the Limit Bid to the Risk Bid on a positive Spade Trump hand with Spades Double. Today, in games where Hearts Triple has become the vogue, still more liberal terms are possible.

Naturally, what goes for Spades Double goes for Hearts Triple. Just say "Hearts" as well as "Spades" and you have it. In fact, with Hearts a sure Trump, a Risk Bid offers more profit in the long run than a Limit Bid in Clubs or Diamonds.

Take the hand just given: If the long suits were Spades and Hearts (instead of Diamonds) you'd have a 2 to 1 cinch if you filled Spades and a 3 to 1 if you filled Hearts. Calling it a 2½ to 1 shot, it would be a good bid.

In all this, however, the Limit Bid is safer, surer in the long run than the Risk Bid. When playing Spades Double and even Hearts Triple, you will win more hands with the Limit Bid than the Risk Bid; and still more with the Sound Bid than the Limit Bid. That is, provided you can get in your quota on a Sound Bid basis. If not, you'll have to step up to the Limit Bid and to the Risk Bid where "doubles" or "triples" warrant it.

As a still longer shot, we have:

## THE WILD BID

This is a great bid—for other players to make. It represents the height of a lot of things, including foolish bidding. With the "Wild Bid" you have just one chance of filling a hand and the classic example is:

| 10 ◇ | 10 ◇ | K ◇ | Q ◇ | J ◇ | J ◇ | 9 ◇ |
|------|------|-----|-----|-----|-----|-----|
| A ♣ | K ♣ | Q ♣ | | | | |
| A ♡ | Q ♡ | | | | | |
| A ♠ | Q ♠ | Q ♠ | | | | |

Here's a hand good for 100 Points in play, with a Meld of 80 for Double Pinochle, 60 for Four Queens, 50 for Royal Marriage and Dix, with 20 for a Common Marriage. Added up, it comes to a Sound Bid of 310, but look at what just one card—the Ace of Diamonds—would do!

It would boost Trumps by 110 through a Sequence and add 100 for Four Aces. There's a bid of 520 right there! It would mean discarding the King of Clubs and breaking up its marriage, but that's a mere 20 Points. It's more than made up by the added playing value of the Ace of Diamonds, which also adds to Trump length.

Actually, this hand is worth just what it shows right now: 320 as a Sound Bid. It's about a 5 to 1 chance that the Ace of Diamonds won't be in the Widow, so the bid is no good. You'd need Spades Double and Hearts Triple, both at once, to make that worth while and there is no such animal.

Many players just can't resist the sight of a mess like this. They forget what a Sound Bid is—if they ever knew—and start bidding up to 400. They'll keep on from there, too, weighing every bid as if they had a chance, which they haven't.

There's no "in between" with such a hand. If you want to be a sure loser in a Pinochle session, go after "one fill" prospects. That will do it.

The only time to bid such a hand is with:

## THE BLUFF BID

Actually, with the "Bluff Bid," any hand will do. If you bid it with a Risk Bid hand or with a Wild Bid hand, it is better than bidding it with nothing—which you may also do when necessary.

The purpose of the Bluff Bid is to force other bidders up in a game where they are already bidding too high or going for Wild Bids. It's like a bluff in Poker, or certain other games, a necessity in some sessions.

Judgment must be used with the Bluff Bid, so there is no fixed rule regarding it. But it's particularly good when playing with two brisk bidders who are both apt to go overboard. In that case, you can speed matters by staying in the bidding yourself—even with nothing —just long enough to help them get higher than they should be.

If you feel the need for a Bluff Bid is merely occasional, reserve it until you are holding a hand with a good potential Risk Bid or even a Wild Bid. Still remember that your purpose is to bluff and pull out if you can. But if you do get hooked, there's still a chance that the Widow may fill your hand so you can play it.

There are hands, however, that are made to order for a Bluff Bid, even though they can't be filled, as:

| A ♠ | A ♠ | 9 ♠ | 9 ♠ |
|-----|-----|-----|-----|
| K ♡ | K ♡ | 9 ♡ | 9 ♡ |
| Q ♣ | Q ♣ | 9 ♣ | 9 ♣ |
| J ♢ | J ♢ | 9 ♢ |     |

This is a really wonderful hand. It's good because there's practically nothing there to fill. It's good because it's no good—and neither are the other hands, though the people holding them won't know it.

With this hand, you have "doubles" in every suit. The Aces block a run in Spades; the Kings in Hearts; the Queens in Clubs; the Jacks in Diamonds. Nobody can fill Four Aces, Four Kings, Four Queens or Four Jacks. Nobody can even get a Pinochle—except you.

They may have Marriages; that's all. But better still, their hands may be replete with possibilities. Anything they will really need may be in the Widow, so they think, but actually you're holding it. If you start this off with a 300 bid, another player is almost sure to raise it. You can pull out right then and there, because he won't make it.

It's nice when two players bid themselves up higher from that point on. So watch for these hands with doubles. They're devils, where Pinochle is concerned.

That sums the substance of bidding; next we come to Pinochle Play.

# PARTNERSHIP PINOCHLE

This is usually a four-handed game, similar to the old three-handed pastime but with a partnership feature. Four hands are dealt, 12 cards to each player and the final card is turned up as Trump.

Players then Meld and go for Points in play, the object being to reach 1000. But instead of playing individually, they form two teams, the opposite players being partners in the game.

However, the Melds are individual; that is, one player can not add his cards to his partner's Meld.

The simple Auction feature is often used in Four-handed Pinochle and adds zest to the game. If a team fails to make its bid, that amount is deducted from the score, as in the Three-handed game.

In recent years, Six-handed and Eight-handed Pinochle have been introduced as partnership games. In Six-handed, there are three teams, each consisting of the two players seated opposite. In Eight-handed, there are four teams.

In both of these games, a 96-card pack is used—consisting of two Pinochle packs—so in Six-Handed, each player is dealt 16 cards and in Eight-handed, each receives 12 cards. Special values may be given to certain Melds such as Triple Pinochle or a Dozen Aces, but these are seldom used in serious play.

## Chapter VII

## HOW TO PLAY THE HAND

The ideal hand in Auction Pinochle is one that contains high, winning Trumps, plus plenty of extras, as well as the top cards of a Second Suit, with a few additional. As an example:

| A♠ | A♠ | 10♠ | K♠ | Q♠ | Q♠ | J♠ |
| A♦ | A♦ | 10♦ | 10♦ | J♦ | J♦ | |
| J♣ | | | | | | |
| J♡ | | | | | | |

The proper play with this hand would be to "clear" the Trumps, keeping a few to make sure of Last Trick. Then "clear" the Second Suit and play it out completely.

You have seven Trumps so you know there can only be five against you. Play of the Ace, Ace, Ten may capture all five Trumps that the opponents hold between them. If it doesn't, it still may take in an opponent's Ten, making your King good. Should the Ten still be out at the end of the third play, force it with a Queen.

Now play the Second Suit (Diamonds) in the same fashion. Whether you can make both Jacks of Diamonds depends a lot on how the opposing cards lie. This hand is rather close to automatic, as you will have shown most of your cards in the Meld, which totals 270 and it's good for 170 in the play. It's better than 400, should make 440 and could score 480.

A really strong hand should have winning cards and length besides. With two Aces, you need eight or more cards in the suit. With two Aces and a Ten, you need seven, though six will often do. Two Aces and two Tens are plenty high—but they need those two (or more) extra cards for length!

Take a hand where Trumps have high cards plus length, but the Second Suit has length alone:

| A♡ | A♡ | 10♡ | K♡ | Q♡ | J♡ | 9♡ |
| A♣ | K♣ | K♣ | Q♣ | Q♣ | 9♣ | |
| Q♦ | | | | | | |
| Q♠ | | | | | | |

In this case, start with the Second Suit (the Clubs). Pick up what tricks you can at the start. Here, you have only one sure trick, the Ace of Clubs. Play it, then work up in Clubs, using a Queen to force the opposing Tens and Ace.

Your purpose is to establish this Second Suit for whatever it can bring in. The opponents will come back in Diamonds or Spades, which you can trump after the second play in either of those suits. Then go after Clubs again, forcing what you can. Once you've established Clubs, clear your Trumps (Hearts) and whatever Clubs you have left can be made good. It's that simple.

But here is something more complex:

| A♣ | 10♣ | K♣ | Q♣ | J♣ | | |
| A♡ | A♡ | K♡ | Q♡ | J♡ | J♡ | 9♡ |
| A♠ | Q♠ | | | | | |
| J♢ | | | | | | |

This is a very common type of hand, wherein Clubs became Trump because it showed a Sequence—nothing else. The Second Suit (Hearts) is long, with only two top cards. The logical play would therefore be:

Lead the Aces of Hearts; next, the small cards from that long Second Suit. The idea is to make them play out their high Hearts, which will make your King and remaining Hearts good. Or you may force one opponent to trump your low Hearts, which may give you a chance to clear Trumps by leading them.

Much depends upon the Second Suit in a hand like this. The important points are: You are out to get all you can from it, but at the same time, you are using it—or sacrificing it—to make up for your shortage in Trumps.

In a hand like this, the lead of a very minor card—such as a Jack of Hearts—might force both opponents to play Trumps, which in turn would enable you to clear Trumps.

One important rule to remember: You must clear Trumps or take the final Trump in order to pick up that often all-essential Last Trick.

Sometimes a balanced hand of three suits may be held, as:

| A♡ | 10♡ | K♡ | Q♡ | J♡ |
| A♠ | A♠ | K♠ | Q♠ | Q♠ |
| A♢ | K♢ | Q♢ | J♢ | J♢ |

Here, Hearts are Trumps, with Spades the Second Suit because of its winning cards. But where length is concerned, Spades have no edge over the third suit, Diamonds.

As Trumps are comparatively weak, you lead the Ace of Spades, top card of your Second Suit. Suppose a Ten of Spades falls from one opponent's hand.

You are in a dilemma. A lead of the second Ace of Spades might capture the second Ten. But suppose one player is actually out of Spades. Your Ace will be trumped and the other opponent will have one more card than you in your "long" Second Suit.

So you would do well to switch to Diamonds as your "Second Suit, leading the Ace and then leading from the bottom up in that same suit, Diamonds. This will force the Spade lead onto your opponents, giving you a chance to see how things stand in that Suit.

This brings up the almost obvious fact that there are times when it is advisable to lead from a low, weak suit, dropping tricks which the opponents will be sure to take anyway, but gaining a "feeler" through those losses. However, too many players use that procedure habitually and suffer from it.

Your fundamental aim is to clear out Trumps and at the same time control them; then to establish a strong Second Suit. If you lack enough strength in Trumps to do that, throw the burden on the Second Suit. Should it appear too weak, use other measures to bolster it.

In the bidding systems given in this book, special value has been given to added cards in any Suit. The reader can now appreciate why. The more "extras," the more tricks you can take at the crucial final portion of the play.

While you must watch the fall of opposing cards in order to play your hand to best advantage, or to pull through an emergency, there is no reason to go into complicated preliminary calculations as to the percentage "for" and "against" all the Trumps or some special Suit being in one opponent's hand.

That's something you can't help, nor will the bidding tell you, as Pinochle bids are "blind" where naming Trumps are concerned. What's more, those "percentages" have all been figured in our systems. Add up the Playing Value as advised in previous chapters and you will find that allowance has been made for adverse "breaks" to a very definite degree, thus simplifying the entire operation.

Bidders should always remember to profit by mistakes of the opposing players, when they are "paired" against him. To do this, it is important to study the style of play used by opponents, so that over the long run you can afford to take certain chances in the play. Also, knowledge of another player's foibles will help you when you are teamed with him against a bidder.

It doesn't help to tell a player how he should play. If he believes you, he probably won't thank you. More wrangles occur over the Pinochle table for this cause than for all others combined. All such disputes could be and should be avoided. The poorer or more indifferent the opposition, the better it is for the good Pinochle player in the long run.

This proves itself when:

## PLAYING AGAINST THE BIDDER

With many players, this is strictly an automatic process. They throw non-counters when the bidder is sure to take a trick; they throw on counters or "schmeer" those tricks which they feel sure their partner will win.

They usually have sense enough to lead and play non-counters or cheap cards in suits which they know the bidder will be forced to Trump; that is, when he is out of those suits.

Often, a smart bidder can take advantage of the opponent who is over-inclined to schmeer. For example:

Assume the bidder to be holding the King, King and Jack of Hearts. Out against him are the Ten and Queen of Hearts, both held by a player who loves to make his "counters" good as quickly as he can. The third player now has no Hearts, so is due to play one of the few Trump cards he holds, should a Heart be led.

The bidder leads the Jack of Hearts. The opponent plays the Ten. The third man takes it with a Trump. The bidder later regains the lead, clears Trump and both his Kings of Hearts are sure winners, counting 10 Points each by the popular Simplified Count.

Now suppose the second player had simply put the Queen on the Jack that the bidder led. The second player's Ten of Hearts would still have been good; it would have captured one of the bidder's Kings; the third player, out of Trump by then, might possibly have added a schmeer.

In brief, the opponents might have picked up 30 Points instead of only 10, enough to sink the bidder in many instances.

This is one reason why in close, fast Pinochle play, keen watching of counters becomes essential. It's why players accustomed to one form of count run into snags when playing in company that utilizes another style, as mere "fractional" counters can be the difference.

Here, however, are the essentials of play that will enable you to stop the bidder with those few additional points:

Study the bidder's meld, checking any cards that are likely to lose tricks for him during the play. Have counters ready to play on those, whenever possible, unless:

When you are sure a counter can be used to take another trick, bringing in more counters, save it for later use. This applies to a "schmeer" as well.

But normally, whenever possible, you should "schmeer" a trick your playing partner is sure to take and even any trick he might take—provided they are counters that the bidder would probably grab.

In leading against the bidder, do not open a fresh suit if you can help it. Throw that burden onto the bidder. If he is out of a suit, lead worthless cards in that suit, to force the bidder's Trumps. However:

You should usually avoid such a lead when your playing partner will also be forced to Trump. Sometimes you can lead a suit which your partner is able to Trump, capturing an Ace or other high card from the bidder's hand, with a Trump that might have been cleared.

Watch for such opportunities and even lead Trumps yourself, when the bidder has only a small quota of points to make. If he's holding back his Trumps, it's because he doesn't want them played that soon. A Trump lead will often disrupt his plan of play and can prove the "long chance" which will keep him from making his bid.

Sometimes, by leading a low, lone Trump, you can not only discommode the bidder, but will find yourself able to schmeer a trick that your partner takes in a suit which you might otherwise have had to Trump.

Keep two things in mind when playing against the bidder: First, that you are trying to break the very plan or pattern that you yourself would follow as a bidder; second, that one "break" may give you and your partner all the points you need.

The pressure is often on the bidder and his opponents, by watching the counters, may be able to grab the few extra points that they need to sink him. This is why we repeat again:

Learn to gauge the play of your opponents; be ready to take advantage of any inherent weakness in that play; and think of Pinochle as a long range game, with profit or loss determined by repeated sessions, not by the outcome of a few individual hands.

## Chapter VIII

## TWO-HANDED PINOCHLE

This is the Old Original, the grand-daddy of the Pinochle family and still the best of the lot, according to its loyal followers. The game is played thus:

The dealer deals two hands of 12 cards each, dealing them by fours. He turns the next card face-up. Whatever its suit, that becomes Trumps and if it happens to be the Dix (Nine of Trumps) the dealer marks up 10 Points for himself on a score sheet.

The rest of the pack, called the "stock," is laid face down, overlapping the turned-up Trump. As the game proceeds, players draw from the stock in a manner soon to be described.

The dealer's opponent plays first. He leads any card he wants from his hand, laying it face up on the table. The dealer plays a card upon it (any card at all—he does not have to follow suit; nor does he have to play a Trump). However, he can trump the trick if he so desires.

An example will clarify all this:

Assume that the Jack of Diamonds has been turned up as Trump.

Suppose that the opponent leads the King of Spades. That card will take the trick, unless:

The dealer plays a higher Spade, namely the Ace or the Ten, or—

The dealer plays a Trump, in this case any Diamond. The dealer then would take the trick.

If the opponent should lead a Trump, such as the Ten of Diamonds, the only way the dealer could take it would be with a higher Trump, which would have to be the Ace.

The dealer may, of course, "throw" on any card he wants, letting his opponent take the trick.

All this is important, because:

The player who wins the trick has the privilege of making a Meld, should he hold such a combination in his hand. He can Meld anything from a simple Marriage up to a Hundred Aces, or even a Roundhouse—if he has it—for 240 Points.

The only thing he would *not* meld at this stage would be a Sequence (150) in Trumps, because in Two-Handed Pinochle it is allowable to Meld a Royal Marriage (40) first and add the remaining cards of the Sequence later, as a new and independent Meld for 150. Done that way, Royal Marriage + Sequence can actually give the player 190 toward his score. But he would have to wait until a later trick to lay down the Ace, Ten, Jack of the Sequence.

Other procedures or limitations affect the Meld, but most of these will be discussed later; that is, in relation to allowable combinations. For the moment, the reader should take particular note of one factor:

The Dix, or Nine of Trump, can be Melded along with any other Meld and in Melding it, the player is allowed to change it for the turned-up Trump beneath the stock.

This has a strong bearing on the play. Suppose, with the Jack of Diamonds turned up as Trump, the dealer finds that he is holding the Nine of Diamonds. He may be very anxious to acquire the Jack of Diamonds. If his hand contains two Tens of Diamonds, he might use one to Trump the opponent's lead, in order to Meld the Dix and pick up the Jack.

Similarly, if his opponent held the Dix, the opponent might make a strong lead—even the sure-win Ace of Diamonds, if he held both —in order to pick up the Jack. On the contrary, some players may go on carelessly, trusting that the other does not hold a Dix.

Because, in Two-Handed Pinochle, players are working on possibilities of a most intriguing sort.

After a trick has been taken, the winner draws a card from the top of the stock; that is, the remainder of the face-down pack. The loser then draws a card from the stock. They do this to keep their hands up to a total of 12 cards each.

The winner then leads another card and the loser plays as he pleases, letting the trick go, or taking it if he prefers and can spare a card that will take the trick. Whoever wins can again make a single Meld. The winner then draws a card, the loser draws one, and the play continues.

By now, it is quite obvious that each player should hold on to cards that may be usable in coming Melds. He may even hold some of those Melds already, or he can be building toward some as futures.

As an example: With the Jack of Diamonds turned up as Trump, suppose these hands were held:

### OPPONENT

| K ◇ | Q ◇ | J ◇ |     |
|-----|-----|-----|-----|
| A ♠ | 10 ♠ | K ♠ | J ♠ |
| A ♡ | J ♡ |     |     |
| A ♣ | J ♣ | 9 ♣ |     |

### DEALER

| K ◇ |      |      |     |
|------|------|------|-----|
| K ♠ | 9 ♠  | 9 ♠  |     |
| A ♡ | 10 ♡ | 10 ♡ | K ♡ |
| 10 ♣ | 10 ♣ | Q ♣  | J ♣ |

The opponent has no dix, and he already has a Jack of Diamonds in his hand. However, he has some Melds in hand and some good potentials. He'd like to take this trick without great sacrifice, so he can make an immediate Meld.

As a result, he leads the Ten of Spades. It can't help any Meld and the dealer will be forced to waste an Ace of Spades or a Trump to take the trick. It's a better play than the Nine of Clubs, which the dealer could take with a Ten of Clubs, or even a spare King or Queen. So the dealer is confronted with a problem right away.

Since the dealer has no Dix and no immediate Meld, he tosses on one of his useless Nines of Spades and lets the opponent take the trick.

Immediately, the opponent Melds his Forty Jacks, by placing them face up on the table and marking 40 in his score column. He then draws a card to fill his hand and the dealer the same.*

The reason the opponent prefers Forty Jacks as his Meld, rather than a Royal Marriage, is this:

He is allowed to play cards from his Meld as well as from his hand. Now, of the Four Jacks that he Melded, only one has any future value; namely, the Jack of Diamonds, which will form a Pinochle with a Queen of Spades—if he draws one!—or may eventually be usable in a Sequence.

The other three Jacks, once scored, have fulfilled their function. They become excellent cards for the play. In fact, he leads one—the Jack of Spades—right now. His reason: Since he had one Ten of Spades, the dealer is not too likely to be holding the other. The opponent wants to take another trick.

The opponent takes the trick, the dealer tossing on a worthless

---

*Assume the Opponent draws a Nine of Hearts and the Dealer draws a Nine of Clubs.

Nine spot. The opponent now Melds his Royal Marriage (King and Queen of Diamonds) for 40 Points more. He draws a card from the stock, the dealer draws one and the play continues.

Notice here: If the opponent had led the Jack of Hearts or the Jack of Clubs; in fact, if he should lead one of those cards now, the dealer would logically take the trick with a Ten of the suit led. The dealer could then lead a Ten of the other suit expecting the opponent to throw away a low card.

It's good to have Tens handy as they can often take crucial tricks, but one of a suit is enough and it's better to have none than to have to "throw" one. Such things will be discussed in more detail later. For the present, let's see what happens as the hand is played out.

This business of playing a trick, Melding—when possible—and drawing, continues until the players exhaust the stock; namely, at the end of 12 tricks. By then, some one will have "cashed" the Dix for the Jack of Diamonds.* The winner of the twelfth trick picks up the final face-down card and the loser gets the face-up Dix.

Each player now picks up whatever Meld he has lying on the table, so that the hands consist of 12 cards each with nothing showing and no more cards to draw. In front of him, each player has (face-down) the tricks that he has so far taken.

Now, they play for more, but here the usual Pinochle procedure is invoked:

Whatever card is led by the winner of the previous trick, the other player must follow suit, if he can.

If unable to follow suit, the second player must Trump, if he can; otherwise he may throw any card.

Should a player lead a Trump, the other player must not only play a Trump but must play a higher one, if possible.

At the finish, the two players add up their counters (by whatever scoring system they prefer) including 10 Points for last trick. These are added to the Meld score and the deal goes to the opponent. The game continues with more hands until one player acquires a grand total (Melds and Points) of 1000.

Two-Handed Pinochle is a highly intriguing game, one that taxes both the wits and keen judgment of the players. It must be played to be appreciated and it is one form of Pinochle that requires good "card sense." Here, in brief, are some angles on its play:

_____
*After one Dix has been "cashed" for the face-up Trump, the other can still be declared, along with any Meld, for 10 Points. The declarer retains this Dix.

Your purpose during the first twelve tricks is to Meld as much as possible so watch those prospects from the very start. Suppose, with Hearts as Trump, you should hold:

| | | | |
|---|---|---|---|
| A ♡ | 10 ♡ | | |
| A ♣ | K ♣ | Q ♣ | |
| A ♢ | K ♢ | Q ♢ | |
| 10 ♠ | K ♠ | J ♠ | 9 ♠ |

You already have two ordinary Marriages. By leading the Ten of Spades, you can immediately Meld a Marriage (Clubs or Diamonds) if you win the trick. If your opponent is very eager to take that trick, he might top it with the Ace of Spades. That sounds bad, as it gives him 20 Points (his Ace and your Ten) and enables him to Meld instead of you.

But early in the game, that's helpful. His play of the Spade Ace is almost a sure indication that he holds the other Ace. That makes your prospects of Four Aces nil and tips you off to the fact. Suppose he should then Meld a Pinochle (Jack of Diamonds and Queen of Spades). You'd know that your chance of making a later Meld of Sixty Queens would be considerably lessened, since you would only have one Queen of Spades to draw.

Let's say he should let your Ten of Spades go by, tossing on a Nine. You Meld a Marriage. Then suppose you draw a Ten of Diamonds, which you'll want to keep as a Trump. You would have two "waste" cards, the Jack of Spades (as it's no use trying for Forty Jacks) and the Nine of Spades. So you'd lead the Nine.

It's considered good policy to let your opponent gain and retain the lead during the early tricks as it gives you an inkling of what he holds in Melds and at the same time enables you to build up a strong playing hand for later use. But if you have early Melds to declare, it is best to get them down on the board, particularly when you have additional Melding prospects and are short on cards that you can throw away.

Suppose that with Hearts as Trump, you Meld a Double Pinochle (both Jacks of Diamonds and Queens of Spades). You now have two Jacks of Diamonds that are expendable. If you have no King of Spades, you can afford to toss one of the Queens. This is very helpful if you have no Nines or other cards to throw.

Here's a classic case: You hold an Ace in each suit, a Hundred Aces, right at the start. Should you meld this "biggy" in a hurry or hang onto it?

Hang onto it if it's all you hold in the way of a solid Meld, with few prospects of filling other Melds, and if you have some Tens and Nines, as you probably will have in such a hand. Your Hundred Aces are a sure Meld later and by keeping your opponent in ignorance, you may keep him nursing Aces which he is unlikely to fill, since four are out against him.

But on the contrary: If you have lots of potential Melds (mostly in Kings and Queens) and practically nothing to throw (like Nines and worthless Jacks) you should Meld those Hundred Aces fast. You'll then be able to make other Melds which you already hold or may fill rapidly and you'll have three Aces sitting on the board, ready to take whatever your opponent leads in any Suit, including a Ten. And when you take such tricks, you can Meld.

We've cited this to show why it's impossible to hold to any fixed, fast rule of play. However:

If you want to keep the lead, it's best to play from a long Suit, as the opponent will have less chance to top it. The Ten is usually best, but suppose you should hold both Tens and an expendable Jack, a lead of the Jack might be smart for two reasons:

(a) The opponent isn't likely to top it with a King or Queen that he is saving for a possible Meld.

(b) The opponent won't be tempted to take a Jack with a spare Ace, but he would very likely hit one of your Tens with such an Ace.

To get rid of the lead, you should lead a Nine from a short Suit. Also, in throwing away cards, toss them from a short suit when feasible.

Remember that in throwing weak cards on early tricks, you will be saving stronger ones for later plays when the "stock" is running short. Very important, because:

Chances of "filling" certain Melds increase as the play proceeds and you may often have to win tricks to declare "last minute" Melds.

Get certain Melds in early rather than sacrifice them. Declare a Royal Marriage early—for its 40 points—when you are going after the remaining cards for a 150 Sequence. Late in the play, it is often better to sacrifice a belated Royal Marriage to make sure of the 150 Sequence, which brings up an important fact; namely, that:

Trumps are very valuable as "trick takers" in order to make a "last minute" Meld. Often, a lead of an Ace of Trumps will make such a final Meld possible. Or even better:

A series of strong leads as the stock dwindles may make it impossible for your opponent to declare his late Melds. Keeping his Meld down is just as important as adding to your own, sometimes more so as the game approaches the 1000 mark.

Once you have made a Meld, always play a card from that Meld in preference to a duplicate you may hold in your hand. As an example, suppose that:

You have Melded:     Your opponent has Melded:

J♢  Q♠                        K♠  Q♠

In your hand, you have the other Jack of Diamonds. It's no good to you, since your opponent Melded the Queen of Spades that should go with it. But don't lead the Jack from the hand. Lead the Jack from the Meld.

Your opponent will then continue to think that he may draw the extra Jack of Diamonds to go with his Queen of Spades. He will hang onto the Queen encumbering his hand with a worthless card. He may be forced to throw a Ten on one of your leads or sacrifice a Trump or a small Meld like a Marriage.

This brings up the very important angle of watching your opponent's play. Suppose he should play both Queens of Hearts as the stock dwindles; you can then be pretty sure that he does not hold either King of Hearts and has given up hope of drawing one to make a Heart Marriage.

Now, if you happen to be holding Kings in the other three Suits, but have no King of Hearts, you could hang onto your Kings, hoping to draw a King of Hearts from the stock and make a meld of Four Kings for 80 Points.

As the stock dwindles, give more attention to the playing possibilities of your hand. Make sure that any Ace you are holding has a side-card in that Suit, or your opponent may lead the other Ace and take yours, as the game enters its final stage.

Again, watching your opponent's Melds will give you keys to proper cards to hold. The more Trumps you retain, the better. The player who consistently takes the larger proportion of the counters is apt to win games regularly from an opponent who is careless in that respect.

To clarify the melding procedure in Two-Handed Pinochle, a Table of Melds is given on an accompanying page, illustrating the various Melds and placing them in separate categories or types, as a convenient way of recognizing which Melds can—or can not—be declared when utilizing cards that have figured in a previous Meld.

Note that *Double Pinochle* is considered as a single Meld. Once it was worth 300, and fairly enough, as a player had to acquire all four cards to make it. Today, this rather freakish value has been discontinued by most players, so that Double Pinochle scores only 80, the equivalent of two ordinary Pinochles. But that is no reason to deprive it of its status as an individual Meld. Anyone holding it can Meld it all at once for 80 Points.

Similarly, Grand Pinochle: King, Queen of Spades and Jack of Diamonds, while now only rating 60 Points (except when Spades is Trumps) is regarded as an individual Meld by many veterans of the game. Here, again, there is nothing to warrant any change from its one-meld status.

In the final stage of the play, after the stock has been exhausted, a player was originally required to top his opponent's lead in any Suit, as well as Trumps. Some old timers adhere to that procedure today and there is no reason why newcomers should not do the same.

After all, Pinochle is Pinochle—even though it is sometimes called Binocle. The merit of the original game made it the heritage of the present generation and the closer it stays to the original pattern, the longer it will probably last. But all players are entitled to their own opinions, so any changes or local rules may be introduced as desired.

But there are no "Laws of Pinochle," no matter who says so, unless it's the Supreme Court—and even then, there is always the chance of a minority opinion.

## Chapter IX

## RUMMY AND GIN RUMMY

Rummy is played with a regulation pack of 52 cards, but it resembles Two-Handed Pinochle because it is a series of "draws" and "melds"—or "spreads" as they are often called. Taken in its simple, two-handed form, Rummy proceeds as follows:

Ten cards are dealt to each player, one card at a time. The next card is turned face-up beside the pack. This is called the Upcard. The remainder of the pack stays face down, as a stock. Suppose two hands to be:

### OPPONENT

| | | | |
|---|---|---|---|
| K♡ | Q♡ | 9♡ | |
| K♠ | 7♠ | 6♠ | 4♠ |
| K♢ | 10♢ | | |
| 10♣ | | | |

Each player's purpose is to "meld" or discard groups of cards, composed of:

### DEALER

| | | | |
|---|---|---|---|
| J♡ | 6♡ | 5♡ | 4♡ |
| 8♠ | A♠ | | |
| Q♢ | A♢ | | |
| 2♣ | A♣ | | |

Three or four cards of the same value, as:

K♡  K♠  K♢  +  K♣

Or a sequence of three or more from one Suit:

7♠  6♠  5♠  +  4♠  +  3♠  +  2♠

Play begins by the Opponent drawing a card, adding it to his hand to make 11 cards in all. He may either pick up the Upcard, or draw the top card from the face-down stock.

In the sample hands shown, suppose the Opponent should draw

the Five of Spades. He could promptly Meld his three Kings and the Spade Sequence from Seven down to Four.

Following his Meld, he discards, putting his odd card face up on the original Upcard (or beside the pack) so that it becomes the new Upcard. In this case, the Opponent would probably discard the Queen of Hearts, as it can no longer figure in a sequence with the King.

It is then the Dealer's turn.

For his draw, he might pick up the new Upcard, the Queen of Hearts, as it goes toward three Queens or toward a sequence (with the Jack).

The Dealer then Melds his Six, Five, Four of Hearts as a sequence and his three Aces as a trio.

He may also "lay off" cards, if he can, by attaching them to a Meld already made. In this case, he could "lay off" the Eight of Spades as the top end of his Opponent's sequence. After that, the Dealer would discard the Two of Clubs.

The hands would then stand:

OPPONENT

9♡    10◇    10♣

DEALER

Q♡    J♡    Q◇

MELDED CARDS

| | | | | |
|---|---|---|---|---|
| K♡ | K♠ | K◇ | | |
| 8♠ | 7♠ | 6♠ | 5♠ | 4♠ |
| 6♡ | 5♡ | 4♡ | | |
| A♠ | A◇ | A♣ | | |

As play proceeds, any time the Opponent draws a Ten, he can Meld three Tens, throw down the Nine of Hearts (or whatever odd card he may be holding) and declare that he has gone "Out."

Similarly, the Dealer, by drawing a Queen, could Meld all three, discard the Jack and declare "Out." But the Dealer has an added chance: If he should draw the Ten of Hearts, he could Meld his Queen, Jack, Ten as a sequence, discard the Queen of Diamonds and be "out."

In actual play, it is rarely quite that simple. Usually, players **draw lots of cards** they don't want and keep tossing them away.

Also, they frequently prefer to get rid of high cards and go after low ones, for a very good reason; namely:

When one player goes "out" he scores or is paid off according to the number of points showing in the other player's hand. Court cards count 10 each; others, according to their value from Ten down to Ace, which is 1.

In the hands shown:

If the Opponent had "gone out" with the Dealer holding the two Queens and the Jack, the Opponent would have won 30 Points.

Vice versa, if the Dealer had "gone out" leaving the Opponent with the two Tens and the Nine, the Dealer would have won 29 Points.

Theoretically, a player could be so "loaded" with high cards that he could be hit for 100 Points in a single hand. More often, he is "caught" with something like a Two and Ace of Diamonds, so he only loses 3 Points.

Rummy may be played with 3 or 4 players (dealing 7 cards to each) or with 5 or 6 players (with each being dealt 6 cards). The game has many variations, one being to hold a hand until it is completely filled and then "Go Rummy" which means to Meld it all at once. A player doing this collects a bonus, usually double the usual amount, as a reward for the risk he ran.

Rather than enumerate all such variants, we shall go into the details of that highly-popular two-hand game:

## GIN RUMMY

This game, originally called "Gin Poker" is played by two persons as follows: Ten cards are dealt singly to each player, with an Upcard placed beside the pack. If the Opponent refuses to pick up the Upcard, the dealer is given that privilege, thus actually starting the play, unless he too refuses to take the Upcard.

From then on it's played like Rummy, drawing, discarding, going after sets or sequences. But there are no Melds until the finish and the purpose is not just to fill the sets, but to reduce the value of the extra cards to a score of 10 or below.

Here we show two hands: One, the opponent's which has achieved that aim; the other, the dealer's, which hasn't gotten that far:

## OPPONENT

K♡  K♠  K◇  9♠  8♠  7♠  6♠  5♠  4♣  A♠

## DEALER

J♥   10♥   9♥   7♥   2♦   2♥   2♣   2♠   6♣   5♣

We shall presume that the Opponent just discarded a Queen of Diamonds (10) thus chopping his "deadwood" as unmatched cards are called, from a total of 15 to 5, as represented by the Four of Clubs (4) and the Ace of Spades (1). He lays that Queen *face down*, to indicate that this is no usual discard but that he intends to "knock" or show his hand as is.

He then Melds his hand as follows:

K♥   K♠   K♦                                    4♣
9♠   8♠   7♠   6♠   5♠                          A♠

The two unmatched cards are laid to one side, where they are added and count against him, in this case to a total of 5 Points.

Since the Opponent has "knocked" the Dealer now can Meld. He would lay down his hand as follows:

J♥   10♥   9♥                                    7♥
2♦    2♥   2♣   2♠                               6♣
                                                 5♣

The Dealer is stuck with a total of 18 Points. Subtracting the Opponent's 5, that makes a total of 13. So the Opponent is credited with 13 Points for that hand. Game is 100 (or more) Points + a Bonus of 100 for winning the game. However, each player is entitled to 20 Points for each hand that he won during the game.

But there is more to Gin than just that.
Suppose the Dealer's hand had been a little different as to its deadwood; namely:

## DEALER

J♥   10♥   9♥   10♠   2♦   2♥   2♣   2♠   4♠   A♣

If this were Rummy and the Dealer had Melded all he could during the play, he would be stuck with the Ten and Four of Spades and the Ace of Clubs. But in Gin, he is allowed to "lay off" whatever cards he can onto his Opponent's Meld, so instead of being caught with 15 Points, he adds his Ten of Spades to the top of his Opponent's sequence and his Four of Spades to the bottom, so he has only the Ace of Clubs left.

10♠   9♠   8♠   7♠   6♠   5♠   4♠

Dealer's Deadwood:
A♣

Opponent's Deadwood:
4♣  A♠

Here, the Dealer has undercut the Opponent's score by 4 Points. So the Dealer wins the hand and is given an additional 10 Points bonus. In the case of two hands ending in a tie score, the man who "knocked" is loser and the other Player scores 10 Points. In short, the burden of the "win" is placed upon the player who "knocks."

If a player wishes, he can go for "Gin"—which means filling the hand completely before the "Knock." This, of course, usually takes longer and therefore adds a risk. But it has two advantages:

First, a player receives an added bonus of 20 Points for the Gin Hand.

Second, though the other player may manage to unload all his deadwood, the Gin Hand still is winner.

In scoring, the Points that hinge upon the play itself go toward the 100 count. The 20 Point bonus for each hand won, is added afterward. So, of course, is the 100 Point bonus for game itself. If a player scores a shutout game; that is, 100 Points or more to his opponent's 0, the winner gets an extra 100 Point bonus (namely 200 in all) and the loser is said to have been "Schneidered."

There are variations in scoring, some circles giving 25 Point bonuses instead of only 20 for Gin and for each hand won; also, 20 or 25 Points instead of 10 for undercutting the knocker.

Now as to the play itself: Reams of advice could be written, hundreds of illustrations could be given and it all would boil down to one fact:

If you can't remember the discards, as well as any Upcards your opponent snatches up, you shouldn't play Gin Rummy. In fact, maybe you shouldn't play any card games.

Added to that: Unless you can form simple, obvious deductions and to a degree visualize the other player's hand, you will have no use for Gin. The game, not the drink.

There is no use of going into exhaustive computations that every fourth grade schoolboy should know. The fact that it's all pretty simple arithmetic is what has made Gin Rummy so popular. It's obvious that all cards have equal chances of being used in any trio, as Three Kings, Three Queens, etc. The same applies to Four of a Kind.

But in 3-card sequences, there is a difference. A King can only figure in one sequence:

K♠  Q♠  J♠

A Queen, however, can figure in two such sequences, the one just shown, plus the following:

$$Q\spadesuit \quad J\spadesuit \quad 10\spadesuit$$

While a Jack can figure in three, those shown above and this one:

$$J\spadesuit \quad 10\spadesuit \quad 9\spadesuit$$

So on, right down the line, every card has the same prospect as the Jack, even to the Three, which has these possibilities:

$$5\spadesuit \quad 4\spadesuit \quad 3\spadesuit$$
$$4\spadesuit \quad 3\spadesuit \quad 2\spadesuit$$
$$3\spadesuit \quad 2\spadesuit \quad A\spadesuit$$

Note, however, that while the Three of Spades can figure in three 3-card sequences, the Two is limited to two (like the Queen) and the Ace is limited to one (like the King.)

As a result, the Kings are usually the cards that nobody wants and Queens are not too popular. Jacks and Tens, while they rate 10 Points against you, offer sufficient combinations. Threes, of course, are a good bet, so good that a player wants them even if they won't fit in a combo. They help you to "knock" and Twos are even better, with Aces better still, where the "knock" is concerned.

That, plus remembering, adds up to the essence of Gin. Before going into other angles, take the matter of memory:

The best system in Gin is the zest of the game itself. You want certain cards and from a careful study of your hand, you can figure a few that your opponent probably won't want. If you hold the Kings of Spades, Clubs and Diamonds, plus the Queen and Jack of Hearts, it's a foregone conclusion that your opponent won't be happy with the King of Hearts.

He can't possibly have anything to go with it, so it's one of the first things he would discard. If he doesn't discard it, you can be pretty sure it's in the stock. If you don't draw it, your opponent is apt to drop it like a hot potato if he picks it up, so you'll get it then.

Often, discards form a pattern. Your opponent may discard a Ten, then shortly after throw another and finally a third, showing that he began drawing them too late. But this tells more: It indicates that he's not after sequences involving any of those three Tens.

Particularly remember what your opponent picks up and keep watching for tell-tale discards later. For instance: He picks up the

Seven of Clubs. He wants it either for three Sevens or for a Sequence. Which? You watch and see. A little later he discards the Eight of Clubs. It's pretty obvious he filled his Sevens, because he's chucking a sequence card.

Or a tip-off might come from him discarding a Six of Hearts. This shows he may have filled Sevens and therefore has abandoned the idea of adding an Eight or Five of Hearts to a Six and Seven that he held.

Fundamentally, a player should hold onto low cards, not only because he loses less if "caught" with them (as in any type of Rummy game) but because in Gin, such low cards will give him a quicker opportunity to "knock."

It's good policy to knock by the fifth draw, if you can, as you have a good chance of catching your opponent with a lot more than 10 Points in his hand. But by the sixth or seventh draw, it may not be so safe. You'd better get your score down to less than 5 Points. Often, this is a time when you might go for Gin, as with this hand:

$$Q\diamond \quad Q\heartsuit \quad Q\clubsuit \quad 8\clubsuit \quad 7\clubsuit \quad 7\spadesuit \quad 6\spadesuit \quad 5\spadesuit \quad 4\spadesuit \quad 3\spadesuit$$

Three cards will enable you to "knock," namely:

$$Q\spadesuit \quad 8\spadesuit \quad 2\spadesuit$$

By filling with any of these, you can discard the Eight of Clubs, leaving yourself with only the Seven of Clubs as a count.

But there are four other cards that will enable you to make Gin:

$$9\clubsuit \quad 6\clubsuit \quad 7\heartsuit \quad 7\diamond$$

Draw one of those and you either fill a new sequence (three Clubs) or land yourself three Sevens. So Gin you go and it's worth the risk if you think you'd be undercut on that 7 point count.

Remember, too, that if you do draw the needed Queen or high (Eight) or low (Two) Spade of your sequence, you can discard the Eight of Clubs, anyway. You'll still be working toward a Gin and if your opponent should "knock" immediately afterward, you still have only the 7 Points that you'd have been hooked with if you'd "knocked" on your own.

Now, as to the matter of your discards, a problem which confronts the Gin player the moment he picks up his hand. With the early discard, it is obvious that since the player is anxious to accumulate helpful low cards, he should get rid of high ones—provided of course that they are in no way helpful toward a Meld.

Take this hand:

K♣    10◇    8♡    7♡    7♣    5♠    4♡    4♣    3♣    2◇

The obvious discard is the isolated King of Clubs, which is a good reason not to throw it while you have a discard like the Ten of Diamonds, which is equally bare of possibilities.

True, the King can only fit in one possible sequence, whereas a Ten may fit in three. But none of those are in the making and the chances are that you will be throwing the Ten soon, anyway.

If you throw the King now, you'll be doing just what your opponent would probably do. If you sit tight, he may throw one and you can pick it up.

Picking up a discarded King is considered a smart play later in the hand, when you want your opponent to think that you are after high cards—not low. It's a form of "bluff" that helped Gin gain its old original name of "Gin Poker." But it will ring hollow if you've thrown a King to start things.

If you throw the Ten and your opponent picks it up, you'll have a quick line on what he's after. If he lets it ride and draws from the stock, it tells you something too. This isn't advice, it's an analysis. In Gin, you have to analyze all situations and then give yourself advice.

Some players pick up any low discards, figuring that whatever an opponent doesn't want may be good for the player himself. This at least is in keeping with the principal of acquiring low cards for "knocking" purposes. It may also mean that the stock still contains some nice low ones that may be drawn to go with the pickup.

An argument in favor of holding certain high cards, most specifically an isolated King or Queen, is this:

Suppose you are sure your opponent has the other three of that value, say three Queens. He may have picked one up and discarded a high sequence card (like a Jack) that would go with it. If you discard your Queen, you'll be giving him the very card he may need to "knock." But:

If you hold it and he does "knock," you can "lay off" your Queen on his set. When your own hand is near the "knock" stage too, that little device may give you an undercut and a won hand.

All this has to do with the element of "bluff" that becomes important as the game proceeds. A pattern player who is always "Ace Hungry," gets typed for exactly that. Still, a player must follow all the dictates of common-sense. One of these is to discard "dead" cards rather than "live" ones.

At the start of a hand, all the cards are "live." As an example, take the Eight of Hearts. It can combine with two other Eights to form a trio, or it can fit into three possible sequences involving either the Nine of Hearts or the Seven of Hearts.

Now, suppose that in the course of play, two of those other Eights have been discarded and that both the Nine and Seven of Hearts have gone into the discard. The Eight of Hearts is then deader than any door-nail, as there's no way to hook it up with anything. It's fine for you to discard.

Better still: Suppose you've been holding both the Nine of Hearts and the Eight of Hearts, hoping for the Ten (because the Seven has already been discarded.) Suppose you also are holding the Nine of Clubs and you have just drawn the Nine of Spades.

You now have three Nines. You can't use the Heart Sequence. You've taken the Nine of Hearts out of circulation, but your opponent doesn't know it. It's a "dead" card alright, but he might possibly pick it up, thinking it might go with the Jack and Ten of Hearts, should he be holding them.

But in discarding "deaders" you are banking more on thwarting your opponent than you are on bluffing him. By watching the discard, your opponent's pickups and checking your own hand, you can often feed your opponent "dead" cards right along, or those that are half-dead, or more.

In the case of the Eight of Hearts, if two other Eights were still unaccounted for, the card would still be "dead" as far as sequences were concerned. If you were sure that the fourth Eight had been buried, the Eight of Hearts would be partly dead in that department, too.

Similarly, if you were holding the Nine of Hearts and the Six had been discarded, the Eight would be dead from the sequence standpoint. Again, your opponent would be nicely ignorant of the fact. Even though he knew the Six was gone, he wouldn't know you held the Nine.

That is, not unless he figured you for it. Part of the game is just that. The game was invented too late for Sherlock Holmes to play, but he would have liked it from the standpoint of deduction. So be your own Sherlock and try it for yourself.

## NO. 710

**A**—Enlarged Diamonds. It is all in one place near left hand side and is considered one of the best combinations on Bee 67. Our Enlarged Diamond work cannot be improved upon.

Per Deck $4.13

## NO. 730

**B**—Small White Diamonds. This is similar to Enlarged Diamonds, but instead of enlarging red or blue diamonds, we reduce the white diamonds.

No. 710 or No. 730   Ace to 8 ............. Deck   3.13
No. 710 or No. 730   Ace to 2 .............. Deck   4.13

## NO. 740

**C**—Double Line Work shows to better advantage than single line work. This is the old reliable, well liked, and a quality of work that no one has been able to duplicate.

No. 740   Reads from Ace to 2 ............... Deck   3.13

## NO. 750

**D**—One side of the white diamond is reduced. Some customers prefer this to small white diamonds. This work sometimes called Neostyle.

No. 750   Reads from Ace to 2 ............... Deck   3.13

Page from a catalog published by a gambling supply house

## Chapter X

## RED DOG AND BLACK JACK

These games will be discussed in a single chapter because they can be handled briefly and also because they have strong points of similarity. They are alike, not only because they are dealing games in which the players bet against the pot, or bank, but in the deadly way they ruin the average person who tackles them.

Also, when chicanery enters, as it so often does, the crooked work utilized in Red Dog and Black Jack is very much the same. That will be explained and detailed in the final chapter, so for the present let us concern ourselves with the actual games. First we shall introduce:

### RED DOG

There is one basic rule to follow in Red Dog. That rule is: "Never bet the pot." That means, in turn, never to make a wager beyond your own set limit, as will be understandable from the game itself. Red Dog, it so happens, is one of the simplest games known.

Each player is dealt a hand of four cards. He then matches these against a card dealt from the top of the pack. If he has a higher card in that suit, he wins. If not, he loses.

Suppose a player should hold these cards:

A♣ 10♣ J♡ 5♠

His hand will then beat any single Club that happens to be dealt. He can also beat any Heart of a value below the Jack and any Spade below the Five. He will lose if any Diamond turns up.

The odds are very simply figured. Since the player holds 4 cards, he must calculate his chances against the remaining 48. In the example given, he can beat any Club, 11 in all. He can beat 9 Hearts, 3 Spades and 0 Diamonds. So there are 23 chances out of 48 that he will win—just barely less than an even chance.

If the player should hold the Six of Spades instead of the Five, his chances would be exactly even.

Here is a quick way of calculating the odds:

75

Count each Ace as 14, a King as 13, Queen 12, Jack 11, Ten as 10 and so on, numerically, down to the Deuce, which rates as 2.

Note the top card of each Suit appearing in your hand. Subtract 2 from its value and add the totals. Subtract 1 for each additional card in any Suit.

In the example given:

Ace of Clubs would be 12 (14 less 2). Jack of Hearts would be 9 (11 less 2). Five of Spades would be 3 (5 less 2). These add up to 24, from which 1 is subtracted (for the additional Club). That gives the player 23 cards to beat.

The following would be a perfect hand:

A♣   A♠   A♡   A◇

Each card is added as 12 (14 less 2) and the total becomes 48 out of a possible 48.

Here is a hand which would be an absolute dud:

2♣   2♠   2♡   2◇

Each card is added as 0 (2 less 2) and the total becomes 0 out of a possible 48.

Here is a sample of a "two-suiter":

A♣   J♠   10♠   4♠

The Ace rates 12 (14 less 2) and the Jack as 9 (11 less 2). From that total of 21, we deduct 2 for the additional cards in the Spade suit. Result: 19 out of a possible 48.

Now for the method of betting the hands:

In Red Dog, all the players first contribute to a "pot" in the center of the table, say one chip each—or whatever number may be agreed upon. This pot is actually like a bank, as the players bet against it—not against each other.

Each player bets from one chip up to whatever number the pot contains. If he wins, he takes out the number of chips that he bet. If he loses, he puts that many into the pot, increasing its size proportionately. To go the limit, a player "bets the pot" and Red Dog then becomes a deadly game indeed.

Suppose that in a game with eight players starting with eight chips in the pot, four players in a row should "bet the pot" and miss. The size of the pot would jump from 8 to 16, 32, 64 and then 128 chips, all in a matter of four wagers, perhaps in a single deal.

With chips rating at 25c, the game would automatically be raised from a mere $2 limit to a $32 limit for anyone daring enough to "bet the pot." This is by no means uncommon in Red Dog, because many players stay with a minimum bet of a single chip, except when they decide to "go for broke." And often they *go broke* in the process.

In fact, the pot can get so big that it is beyond a player's financial capacity to shoot for it. Obviously, the fatter it becomes, the thinner most of the bankrolls will be. When the game ends, the pot is divided equally among the players. Hence they may—by mutual consent—invoke the divvy rule whenever they want.

For instance, when a player wants to leave the game, the only fair thing is to divide the pot and start anew. Or, when practically nobody has any chips left to bet, a divvy can be made and a new pot started on the basis of a chip apiece. This injects new action into the game and Red Dog players crave action. This is highly important as we shall soon see.

All the experts agree that in Red Dog, a player should rate his hand and if his chances are less than even, he should make the minimum bet. But if they're above average, he should bet more— and maybe a lot more, according to how strong those chances seem.

Good advice, so good in fact, that everybody has a better than average chance of winning! One expert advises thus: Bet the minimum (one chip) if the chances are less than even. Make a larger bet when they are better than even (more than 24 out of 48). Bet the pot when they are 2 to 1 in your favor; that is, when your hand will beat 32 out of 48 cards.

A hand consisting of Four Tens would qualify on this basis. So would Three Aces and a Deuce of the odd suit. But you could draw a lot of hands like that and win with most of them, yet *still lose* in a game of Red Dog if you insisted on betting the pot.

In banking games, it isn't *how much* you can *win* or *how often*. It's *how well* you can stand your *losses*. Now, Red Dog is a *banking game* in which all the players happen to be investors and like every bank, it has a *limit*. In Red Dog, the limit *varies*, being determined by the amount of cash in the pot.

No intelligent player would go to Las Vegas and bet $100 at the crap table if the management warned him that his next bet might be limited to a mere $10. How could he hope for a comeback after missing on a few $100 plays?

But the player who "bets the pot" in Red Dog will be doing just that, if he makes such a wager when the pot has reached a size that it is not likely to attain again. Actually, it's not your chance of winning a hand when the chips are down that counts the most. It's how many of those chips you can afford to lose—and still be able to get them back.

So the rule is, "Never bet the pot" except when it happens to be away below average, because your limit should be based on that average. Suppose that it runs consistently above 24 chips.

In that case, you can set yourself a rising scale on the following order:

If your card count is:

> No higher than 24, bet 1 chip.
> From 25 up to 28, bet 4 chips.
> From 29 up to 32, bet 8 chips.
> From 32 up to 36, bet 12 chips.
> From 37 up to 40, bet 16 chips.
> From 41 on upward, bet 24 chips.

Sometimes the betting loosens, with higher stakes the aim. This means that the pot will run a higher average, say 32 or more chips. Then the system player can "up" his own betting scale. It differs according to how "tight" or "loose" the game may be.

There is another point of difference. As the play goes around the table, each man has to match a card dealt specially to him. If you're "under the guns"—that is, next to the dealer—this will have no bearing on your hand. But when you are farther around the table, it can influence your betting.

Suppose you are holding:

$$K\clubsuit \quad 9\clubsuit \quad J\diamondsuit \quad 10\spadesuit$$

This hand has a value of $11 - 1 = 10 + 9 + 8 = 27$. By the betting schedule it would be good for 4 chips. Its score of 27 means that there are 21 cards out that can beat it.

Now, suppose the first player is dealt the King of Spades and promptly throws in his hand without showing it. You know there are now only 20 cards that can beat you and your own hand is worth 28.

Say that the next player is dealt a Jack of Clubs and beats it with the Ace of Clubs. There's two more big ones gone, in the way of cards that can beat you, so it makes your hand worth approximately 30. You would have an 8-chip bet by that time.

Simply add one point to your score every time you see a card dealt or played that is bigger than any you hold.

But the rule also works the other way. Suppose the Four of Diamonds is dealt and a player beats it with the Seven. Both are cards you'd hoped would be dealt to you, as you could beat either with your Jack. They're just as bad as if they'd been in your own hand as extras. So you will have to knock off a point for each card, bringing your count down to 28, again only a 4-chip bet.

Just follow that rule of adding or subtracting points according to whether a card beats you or you beat it. You can then bet accordingly. Actually the difference is seldom of much consequence. The dealer, or last player, has about the same break as everybody else. But it can shift just enough to put the bet in a new category by our system.

Red Dog may be played with five cards dealt to each player instead of only four. This means that Four Aces (plus some odd card) have only 47 cards to beat. A hand that had 23 chances out of 48 would (because of an odd lower card) have 23 out of 47. The difference isn't enough to change your betting plan. So keep to the regular scale.

However, it does improve the hands, giving them a 20% better chance of having cards in all four Suits. This in turn will "up" your betting average.

Now that you know how to play Red Dog—if you can find an honest game—let's move into the subject of:

## BLACK JACK

This game is also known as Twenty-one, a name derived from the French of *Vingt-et-un,* which means the same thing and describes the game to some extent. A regulation pack is used and the cards are valued as follows:

> Ace, 1 or 11, as you wish.
> All Court Cards, 10 each.
> Others, 2 to 10, as per their value

Suits have no recognition in this game, which is a good reason to avoid it as you will learn in the final chapter. For the present, the game itself:

One player acts as dealer. He deals each player a face-down card, with one for himself; then a face-up card to each. The game is now under way. Each player is to receive cards, one by one, as long as he wants them—if he wants any.

You see, the player is after a total of 21, which is why they call it that. Now if he has an Ace (11) and a picture card (10) he already has his 21 and wants no more. If he has two picture cards, totaling 20, he is so close to 21 he will generally want to stay there, because:

If he goes over 21, he has gone "bust," or *a la brassiere,* as they say in French. His hand is no good; it's gone beyond the limit. That makes it a loser. When it happens, the player turns up his cards and pays his bet.

Lots of things can happen. A player with a Six down and a Three up will of course say "Hit me!" Suppose he gets a Four. That's only a total of 13. He has to say "Hit me!", hoping for an Eight, or even a Seven. Instead, he gets a Three. That makes 16, so should he call for another card, running the risk of going bust?

In a pinch he will stay—for one good reason. The dealer has to go through the same process as everyone else. If the dealer goes "bust," everyone who "stayed" will collect. So it is often better to "stay" than risk going "bust."

When the dealer has collected the bets from players who went "bust," he proceeds to deal himself more cards. He may "stay" at 19, for example, which means that he will have to pay off anyone who made 20 or 21. In the case of a tie (in this instance if 19 proved to be another player's total) the dealer is the winner.

Certain procedures should be noted:

In most circles, it is customary for each player to announce his bet before calling for cards. There is a limit on the betting, either set by the dealer or agreed upon by the players before the game commences.

If the dealer finds he has a "natural" combination, consisting of Ace (11) + Picture (10) he immediately announces it by turning up his "hole" card. The combination is unbeatable, so the dealer collects all bets, except:

When another player holds a "Natural 21" it is regarded as a tie, with no payment going to the dealer. In modern play, all ties are frequently put on a "no pay" basis, rather than give the dealer such a strong advantage.

One reason is that in Twenty-One, the dealer retains the deal until some other player comes up with a "natural," when the deal goes to that player. At any time, the dealer may "sell" the deal for whatever price another player is willing to pay for it.

As with other games, Black Jack has quite a few variations, but the more important question is: How can you beat the game, particularly when the dealer is operating on a "tie and win" basis.

A player "under the guns" can figure it thus:

If he has a total of 15, it's about an even chance that he can safely make a draw, particularly when his 15 is made up of two cards that would "bust" him (like a 7 and an 8). So he should risk a draw. But with 16, he has about 8 to 5 against him, so he should hold off.

However, when other players are dealt ahead of you, it will give you an idea of what the dealer may have to do. If they go "bust," you will become the dealer's only target. So study his upcard.

If he has an Ace, Eight, Nine, Ten or face card showing, chances are about even that he can beat your 16, so despite the adverse odds, you may as well call for another card rather than lose as it stands.

However, if they "stay" and are apparently satisfied with what they have drawn, you can often stay with about anything—like 13 or 14—because the dealer may have to draw to beat the other participants. If he is confronted by two or three solid, high-looking hands, he will prefer to take the risk of more than 2 to 1 against him, by drawing if he already has a total of 17.

This gives him a good chance of going "bust" which means that by avoiding that very risk, you have a winning chance proportionately equal to his gamble. So there are times when you can shape the breaks to your own favor.

As a companion to the game of Black Jack, mention should be made of:

## SEVEN-AND-A-HALF

This game hit its early stride in the U. S. A. before Black Jack became popular, though few persons realize it. Only the writer's long experience and familiarity with card games has enabled him to lay a finger on certain facts through observation more than hearsay.

Prior to World War I, the game of Seven-and-a-Half had been introduced in America from back room circles to college dormitories. It was on its way toward gaining a hold in more extravagant if less erudite surroundings and could very logically have become America's Number One game, when General John J. Pershing, popularly known as Black Jack, took the first members of the American Expeditionary Force to France in 1917.

Naturally, the soldiers played their favorite card games, among them Seven-and-a-Half, which was made to order for the lulls in trench warfare. But to play it you had to remove certain cards from the deck, which became inconvenient when the group wanted to switch to Poker, Red Dog, or something of that sort.

Furthermore, the enterprising doughboys, always eager to talk French soldiers into playing cards with them, struck oil when they showed them Seven-and-a-Half. Instead of accepting the American innovation, the poilus exclaimed, "Ah! Vingt-et-un!" They then showed the U. S. troops how Vingt-et-un was played and the Americans obligingly switched to it in order to capture the French trade, as along some sectors of the front, French soldiers were taking green United Cigar coupons with the mistaken notion that they were American dollars.

On that basis, the American players couldn't lose. So they sharpened their skill at Vingt-et-un by playing it among themselves and naturally they translated its name into English and called it Twenty-one.

Later it became popular as Black Jack, but whether that links with Pershing's nickname or was largely coincidence, is something more of interest to entymologists than card players. More important, the soldiers found that it had another advantage over Seven-and-a-Half. Since the entire pack of 52 cards was used, more players could get into a game of Twenty-one than in a session of Seven-and-a Half with its stripped pack of only 40 cards.

So Seven-and-a-Half went into the discard, like the cards it doesn't use, which some folks regard as unfortunate, as they consider it a much neater game than Twenty-one, alias Black Jack. Their logic becomes apparent in studying the game:

Seven-and-a-Half is played with a pack from which 12 cards have first been removed; namely, the Eights, Nines and Tens. It is played much like Black Jack, all the spot cards having their exact value (Ace—1, Two—2, up to Seven—7) and the picture cards rating at ½ point each. The purpose of the player is to acquire cards totaling 7½.

If he goes beyond 7½, he goes bust. If he stops somewhere short, say at 6, 6½ or 7, he must beat the dealer in order to win, exactly as in Twenty-one. The Ace, however, has only a single value—1 Point—and cannot be switched to a different total as in Black Jack.*

*Sometimes a specified face card can be given a "wild" status of anything from ½ to 7. A Joker can also be used as such.

So, superficially, the two games are almost identical, but skilled players promptly recognize the niceties of Seven-and-a-Half as opposed to its clumsy cousin, Black Jack. Though Black Jack allows lots of "stopoff" points between 2 and 21, a player's score may take big jumps because all the face cards count for 10.

But in Seven-and-a-Half, the whole situation is the opposite. Often a player finds he has two court cards to start (each worth ½) so that he has only a score of 1. With ten more pictures in the pack, he still may increase only ½ point on each draw, to 1½, 2, 2½ and so on, though bigger jumps are sure to occur before he reaches 7½.

Often, however, when starting with 1 Point (½ + ½) a player may make a quick jump to, say, 6 (by drawing a 5) and then stage a creep, a ½ point at a time, aiming for 6½, 7, or even 7½. That prospect is tempting in this game, whereas in Black Jack the tendency is to "stay" well below 21, because the prevalent face cards are all 10-point "busters" instead of potential win-makers, as the ½ points are in Seven-and-a-Half.

In a clever creep, a player will study other hands closely to see how many ½ points are showing. Similarly, the dealer has some canny choices confronting him as a lot of face cards may be showing when his turn comes. All this makes Seven-and-a-Half a slower game than Twenty-one, which is why it has failed to regain its popularity among inveterate gamblers.

This applies particularly to the "pros" who know all the angles and some sharp ones with it. They prefer a game that will take your money quicker, as we shall learn in the final chapter.

## RIDER

A--All in left hand corner in one place. Considered the best ever placed on this back. Very good for Stud.

B--Excellent blockout work on the birds. Large and easy to read.

C--Clever Work in flower at side-center of card. Good for Skin.

D--Many prefer this side combination. Also good for Skin.

E--Smart work on the left-hand corner figure.

F--Fine blockout in the flower at end.

G--Excellent combination on the grass in center circle.

No. 403  Rider A-B-C-D-E-F or G ·················· Deck    $3.13

An example of marked cards as offered by a gambling supply house

# Chapter XI

## HOW CHEATS CAN TRIM YOU

This is the most important chapter in the book. It contains loads of advice which on the surface may seem negative because it is of a protective nature; but in the actual process of saving your bankroll it can prove positive indeed.

Start with this: The moment card games begin to be played for stakes rather than amusement, they attract questionable customers or greedy gentry. When you find people who would rather play cards than eat, it's a sound conclusion that you've learned how they do eat; namely, by playing cards.

All surveys of gambling agree that most of its evils are self-induced. There may be little wrong in a friendly card game that involves small wagers, but there can be a lot wrong with certain characters who decide to invade such sessions and garner big money from a lot of trifling bets.

Many light-fingered folk can no more restrain themselves from manipulating cards in a game than they can keep their hands out of other people's pockets in a crowd. As a breed, card sharps and pick-pockets are of a class, with the pickpocket much to be preferred. He at least is honest about having dishonest intentions.

Rather than go into the entire panoply of the phoney Knights of the Card Table, we shall confine ourselves to the practices most frequently used to cheat honest players in Pinochle and the other games described in this book, all of which have points of similarity from the viewpoint of the card cheat.

As to what constitutes a card cheat, that's simple. Anyone who strays one iota from the accepted procedure of a game, comes into that category. If card games are to have laws as well as rules, they must have ethics, too. Anyone who habitually glances at another player's hand without warning him that he is showing it, may not be regarded as a cheat in certain circles, but it's a cinch that he would rather cheat than play fair.

It's like saying that it's alright to take candy from the counter if the storekeeper isn't looking. The next step is to get the storekeeper to look the other way. Similarly, in a card game, a player who likes to glimpse the faces of another person's cards, will start finding ways to tell them from the back—if he can. That pops us right into the subject of:

## MARKED CARDS IN PINOCHLE

What would you think of a game where the "sucker" provided the marked cards or "readers" that would enable a card sharp to trim him? That would be good, wouldn't it?

What's more, suppose that the chump could never prove that he had been cheated because the cards would stand every known test that would prove them to be regulation pasteboards. That would be still better—if it could happen.

Well, it can happen and does happen. Here is the procedure. A game of Pinochle is suggested when no pack is handy. So the cheat asks: "Why not make up a Pinochle pack from two ordinary packs?" If those packs are available, good. If not, the sucker is induced to buy a set of Bridge cards at the corner drug store. That's better than a Pinochle pack because the cards can be used in other games.

So a Pinochle pack is formed, with the top 24 cards from each pack. It differs from a Pinochle pack in one way: The cards have backs of different colors, say half red backs, the other half blue backs. With so many cards—48 in all—this doesn't seem to matter. Not much.

Let's see what a deadly weapon the swindler now has at his disposal. First, in Auction Pinochle, it is customary to spread the cards of the Widow slightly to make sure that only three cards are there.

If all three backs are one color, the cheat knows immediately that there are no duplicates in the Widow. He is sure of three chances for a card he wants; not just two, which sometimes happens.

Another example: The sharpie already holds three Aces—say, Clubs, Hearts and Diamonds, so he wants an Ace of Spades. In arranging his hand, he notes that all three of his Aces have blue backs. The Widow, he notes, has all blue-backers, too.

One thing is certain: If there is an Ace in that Widow, it's got to be the Ace of Spades. The cheat is holding all the other blue-backed Aces. He can't duplicate one of his own unless he picks up a red-backed card.

Where the two-type backs become deadly is toward the end of a hand, when only a few cards remain to be played. It's the cheat's lead and there is a high Trump out against him. The player to his left has been Trumping Diamonds, so a Diamond lead will force that Trump (say a Spade) if that player holds it.

Now, all during the play, the cheat has been watching the backs of the Trumps played and the only one still out has a red back. He notes that the player to his left is holding two red-backers; the other player, two blues. The Trump is where the cheat wants it. He leads a Diamond.

This blue and red back dodge becomes even deadlier in a Two-Handed game. Suppose the cheat is after the King of Spades for 80 Kings. His opponent has already Melded a Spade Marriage, utilizing a King of Spades with a blue back. The cheat, therefore, needs a card with a red back.

If a blue-backed card is on top of the deck, the cheat throws a Nine on the opponent's lead, so the other man will draw that blue-backed card. Should a red-backed card be topping the deck, the cheat would take the trick so as to draw the red-backer.

No need of more examples. These are warnings, not instructions. Naturally, when cheats run in their own crooked packs, they are often marked throughout. This makes the trimming of the sucker a mere matter of course. In Auction, the cheat who knows exactly what is in the Widow can jump to fantastic bids with 100% surety. In the Two-Handed game, he sees everything that's coming up.

## EASY MARKS

In Pinochle, many chumps are easy marks because Pinochle packs are so easy to mark. The reason: The values run only from the Ace down to the Nine. Cards marked with "Special Border Work" are very adaptable to Pinochle. The marks consist in bulges on the borders of the cards—Suits across the top, Values down the side.

With only six Values, these can be restricted to the top half of the card. Similarly, cheats often nick the edges of the cards or apply colored daub (matching the card back) to the required areas. This is called "Marking cards during play."

However, any type of "readers" may be used. Gambling supply houses deliver specially hand-marked packs with regulation backs, at a price of a few dollars per deck. These may be "braced" with heavy lines at places where the cheat knows to look or they may be "blocked out" in certain portions of the design.

Fine "line work," "scroll work" and "shade work" also are specialties of the "artists" who turn out these fixed pasteboards on a wholesale basis in upstairs "shops," to suit all types of games and buyers.

It's usually a case of how good the cheat's eyesight is—or how bad he thinks the chump's may be. The more conspicuous the marks, the easier they are to use; but the same applies to their detection.

## DEALING YOURSELF OUT

In Two-Handed Pinochle, an unwary player can be trimmed on his own deal. That's right, with the cards in his own possession, after he personally has provided a bona fide shuffle, he can sink himself for sure with the first four cards that he deals to his crooked opponent.

To accomplish this, the cards must be trimmed before the sucker. That is, they are special cards that the cheat has purchased from a gambler's mart for that very purpose. The cards have been "trimmed" to narrow size by cutting down their sides a mere fraction of an inch. That is, all the cards except four different Aces.

The Aces have been very carefully cut so they have a slight outward bulge at the center. These are called "bowed" cards or "bellied strippers." The term "strippers" means that they can be stripped from the pack by simply holding one end between thumb and fingers (at the sides) while the other hand slides along the edges of the pack, contacting the bellied cards.

Half-hidden by the cheat's hands, the manoeuver looks as though he were simply cutting the pack and putting the lower section on the top. Actually, he's pulling out four cards—those Aces!—and is putting them on top for the chump's deal.

So the cluck deals his opponent Four Aces on the first round and with that start, hand after hand, it's hard to see how the crooked player can ever lose. It's equally difficult to understand why the so-called Pinochle rules have advocated a "four at a time" deal in the Two-Handed game.

The simple remedy is to deal cards singly or in pairs. That's an option that can be used in any game, if it is properly announced. If you suggest it and some stubborn player demands, "Why do you want to deal that way?" Just tell him: "So I can't cheat you." That should settle it.

In truly dumb circles, cheats introduce common "wedge" strippers into a Pinochle game. These are simply tapered cards and when they are reversed—turned end to end with the others—it is a cinch to pull them out. By reversing Four Aces when gathering up the pack, the cheat can have them all set for his "cut" after the pigeon has completed the shuffle.

Such strippers fail at times when the pack gets shuffled in non-regulation style. But the packs are often marked, too, so the cheat wins one way if he can't another. For years, packs of cards have been sold with marks already printed on them and such cards are usually die-cut to serve as strippers too. But until recent years, the cards were poorly printed and their designs were so odd, that they were apt to excite suspicion except in schoolboy circles.

All that has been remedied. Today, even novelty shops peddle cards with backs resembling standard designs, already marked in manufacture. They aren't regulation packs, but they look it and feel it. They have stripper edges, too, as any one finds who feels for them and the cheat who pays $2 for such a pack may make it back in a single hand.

## THE OLD ARMY GAME

In Auction Pinochle, two sharps can "take" a sucker so easily that they need nothing but a few wits to make up for their lack of scruples. That's why it's never smart to join two strangers in a friendly game; and there are times when two friends may handle you in a strange manner, too. That's why four or five players make up a better Pinochle party.

The two cheats use the Old Army Game, so called, putting the squeeze on their hapless victim. In the bid, they force him to the limit; then signal each other what they hold and proceed to sink him in the play. The pack with two types of backs is a great help in "tipping off the mitt" as the signal system is termed.

By simply arranging the cards in specified clusters, they can tell what they have—or don't have—in the way of needed cards. Other types of signals go with standard packs and there is no need to detail them, as most teams of card sharps use their own.

When one sharp makes a bid, the other also watches for the tip-off. Teamed with the sucker, the second sharp makes false plays or mistakes, so the first sharp wins the hand. Sometimes this excites suspicion, but cheats are always handy with an alibi.

One of the best is to get the chump to play according to a Count with which he is not familiar; say the Old Style, when he has always used the Simplified. When he questions some play, he is told: "You don't understand the count." That is also given as the reason for his consistent loss.

Be wary of slick players who throw that argument at you. If hands are bid soundly or played properly, there is generally a sufficient "safety" margin of 20 or 30 Points—or more. A study of "play results" given earlier in this volume shows that the count seldom varies that much, no matter what style is used.

The deal is a hazard in Auction Pinochle as well as in Two-Handed. When the cards are dished by "threes" a lot can be done with strippers. Also, one dealer always has a partner handy to cut the pack as he wants it.

The moral so far is: Play Pinochle warily and for small stakes, until you are sure you are among friends who are as friendly individually toward you as they are to each other. In Two-Handed Pinochle, avoid strangers and with others, if you have your doubts, buy your own deck and make sure it's a Pinochle deck.

## GIN, THE CHEATER'S DELIGHT

Gin Rummy is truly the cheater's delight, when he can find a sucker, so don't be "it." This, of all games, must be played sociably or not at all.

As in Pinochle, you can be licked before you start in a Gin Rummy game and with your own pack, too. All the cheat does is discard two cards from the pack before the play begins. Often, he simply leaves them in the card case, or slips them back there after th pack has been taken out.

Those two cards are the Nine and Five of Diamonds or the same values of some other Suit. They prove poison to sequences, when sought in that Suit. There are 11 possible 3-card sequences in Diamonds (or any other Suit). These are:

| K-Q-J | Q-J-10 | *J-10-9* | *10-9-8* |
|-------|--------|----------|----------|
| *9-8-7* | 8-7-6 | *7-6-5* | *6-5-4* |
| *5-4-3* | 4-3-2 | | 3-2-A |

The combinations in italics represent those that have been rendered impossible by stealing the Nine and the Five. Cards that would ordinarily appear in three different combos will now only show in one or two —and those are the combos that players go after most.

The cheat, of course, stays away from Diamonds. He feeds those to the sucker, who just gets nowhere. It's hard to hit three Nines or three Fives, too. The cheat avoids those, using them as sucker bait.

Sometimes a Nine is taken from one Suit and a Five from another. Thus the cheat would avoid high Spades (with the Nine absent) and low Clubs (with the Five gone). With two cards gone, the cheat wins rapidly, when the dupe throws him good cards. So the fact that two cards are missing isn't noticed.

But should the game strike a snag and "run out"—that is, use up all the cards in the stock, the cheat still may get by. With two cards gone, the game will finish as it should, with the proper player making the last draw. The sucker may think that the cards he wanted slipped by him in the early discard.

If an *odd* number of cards—say one or three—had been removed at the start, the stock would have come out wrong and that could easily give the trick away.

When the stock runs out, the hand is dead, requiring a new deal. So the cheat gathers the cards quickly and proceeds. If the dupe should suspect that cards were missing, the cheat plays dumb; that's all.

With his own pack, the cheat can employ "readers" with the same deadly results as in Two-Handed Pinochle, as he can tell the top card of the stock by its back just as easily as he can tell the latest Upcard by its face. On every draw he has two cards to pick from whereas the dupe has only one. That gives the cheat a 2 to 1 chance—if he needs it.

## PUSH BUTTON CHEATING

The reason he may not need it is that with unwary players, cheating at Gin Rummy can be reduced to a push-button basis. The sharpie doesn't have to do anything; not even shuffle. That's it: He just doesn't shuffle—at least not enough to matter. But first, he has a little chore to do.

In gathering the cards, he naturally picks them up in Melds from the previous hand. He places these on the bottom of the pack, or the top, as he prefers, remembering their order, such as Four Kings followed by the 10, 9, 8, 7, 6, 5 of Hearts and three Jacks.

If using the dovetail shuffle, the cheat doesn't bother the bulk of this setup. Even with the overhand shuffle, he can cut a top batch to the bottom, or bring the bottom group to the top, without actually doing a "false" or "fake" shuffle. It's just an incomplete shuffle, that's all.

Naturally, a skilled cheat can go into elaborate versions if he wants. The main thing is that when he lays down the pack for his opponent to cut, he knows where about a dozen cards are located—top or bottom —as well as what they are.

An average cut will put a "top stack" down to the middle of the pack. After 20 cards have been dealt and the players have had a few draws each, they will encounter the stacked group. As soon as one card shows, the cheat knows the next dozen that will be drawn, so he plays accordingly—in fact, he may have already started.

A "bottom stack" brings the cards up to about position 14 from the top, when the pack is cut. So the chump will have three or four of those "key" cards in his hand and so will the cheat. The cheat soon gets things he wants from his opponent's discards; or if he doesn't, he knows what his unsuspecting foe is going after. In either case, it's tough on the honest man.

Marked cards, powerful both in Pinochle and Gin, become a "must" to the cheat who hopes to take the Red Dog and Black Jack victims in true professional style. Surprised, you may ask: "But how can 'readers' help the player very much, when the dealer keeps them close in hand?"

They don't. They help the dealer only. So the cheat uses them when working in that capacity. This makes more sense, but still not too much. The backs of the cards may tell the dealer when he's going "bust" but often, if he "stays" as in Black Jack, he may lose anyway.

## THE SECOND DEAL

What he needs is something that will "bust" the other players, either in Red Dog or Black Jack. By using marked cards, he knows whether the top card will ruin or help the sucker. If it will ruin him, the crook merely has to deal it. But if it helps him, what then? Then comes the Second Deal.

The name means what it implies: The second card of the pack is dealt instead of the top one. The mechanics of the manoeuver is this:

The pack is held loosely in the left hand with the thumb resting across the outer end. As the right hand approaches, the left thumb swivels the top card inward very slightly. The right thumb lays itself flat along the outer edge of the pack and draws away the second card, which is promptly gripped by the fingers to complete the deal.

Executed with a normal motion of the hands, this becomes a purely mechanical action, which is why a good "second dealer" is styled a "mechanic" in the gambling trade. The hands conceal the trick move at the crucial moment and nobody can ever prove that the second card was delivered instead of the top one—unless they've been reading the marks too.

Red Dog and Black Jack are murder when the Second Dealer struts his stuff. So don't be a chump, chum. Avoid him. How? By using your own pack, so he won't know the top cards and give you something else? No, that's not the whole answer.

You can still be "moidered" as they now are saying in Los Angeles. The slicker spots the top card with a "shiner"—not the black eye which he deserves, but a tiny mirror that he plants on the table. All he has to do is push the top card a little to one side and the "shiner" will give him a reflection of the index corner. He then proceeds with the "Second Deal," when needed.

The "shiner" may be hidden anywhere: In a match box, a pipe, in a cut-out stack of chips, in a batch of dollar bills, or even in a quill toothpick. The expert usually prefers to have it attached to his hand, so that he can always get the correct angle in relation to the corner of the top card.

As a result, the "Ring Shiner" has become very popular. In its simple form, it is simply a little mirror device that clamps to a finger ring, but in more elaborate form, it is part of a signet ring that can be turned inward into the card sharp's hand and opened up to become a reflector.

Once locked, the ring defies all suspicion. This gimmick is sold at fancy prices by various dealers in gambling appliances. They will even engrave the buyer's initials on the ring, if he wants to be caught with them.